NOW THAT WE'RE MEN

A PLAY AND
TRUE LIFE ACCOUNTS OF
BOYS, SEX & POWER

EDITED BY KATIE CAPPIELLO

dottir
press

NEW YORK CITY

Published in 2020 by Dottir Press
33 Fifth Avenue
New York, NY 10003
www.dottirpress.com

Special discounts are available for bulk purchases by organizations and institutions. Please contact jb@dottirpress.com.

For permission to perform or produce the play *Now That We're Men* in amateur, student, or professional venues, contact Katie.Cappiello@gmail.com or
GoodCapp Arts
200 Atlantic Avenue, #4F
Brooklyn, NY 11201

FIRST EDITION
First printing: December 2019

Design by Drew Stevens

Library of Congress Cataloging-in-Publication Data is available for this title.
ISBN 978-1-9483-4018-2

Distributed to the trade by Consortium, www.cbsd.com.

PRINTED IN THE UNITED STATES OF AMERICA

For my grandfathers,
Cliff Goodwin and Tom Cappiello.

And for Francie.

"Social change is a million individual acts of kindness.

Cultural change is a million subversive acts of resistance."

—Mary Pipher, *Reviving Ophelia*

Contents

Foreword

Marquis Rodriguez

I used to understand systems of oppression as a solid mass, something insurmountable that blocks the way. Blocks the light. They are daunting and they instill fear. What I have learned over time, however, is that these systems are constantly being pushed back, fought out of the way by many fearsome souls who've made it their life's work to push up against these systems until they fall over. Though this is hard and sometimes unforgiving work, they persist.

At around age fifteen, I met Katie Cappiello. She'd invited me to read a piece I'd written about the word *slut*—how and why that word is used against women—after a performance of *SLUT: The Play*. It was immediately apparent what a gift this invitation was. Being exposed to the conversations surrounding Katie's play could not have come at a better time in my life, as I was approaching this idea of manhood and what it would mean for me to become a man. I began to see how connected I was to issues of rape, sexuality, and how boys are taught to be men. Seeing my own reality—seeing the systems I was part of—was crucial to the project of transforming rape culture.

It's not often that you come across art that gives you the *exact* tools you need to do this work yourself—

art that acts as a guide on the long journey to breaking these systems down—but *Now That We're Men* is one of those works of art. In this play, Katie Cappiello gives language to truths that, for reasons lost on me, are largely denied or silenced. This play asks questions I have never heard voiced, much less answered. Questions like: "What have we done to our young men?" "What are we *still* doing?" "How are we going to fix this?" *Now That We're Men* sits the audience in front of a mirror—as all good theatre does—and invites them to really look at themselves, to see their role in the creation of a problem and point them toward how it might be addressed.

In 2018, I traveled with the cast of *Now That We're Men* to Chicago's famed Steppenwolf Theatre to participate in the talk-backs that always follow performances of Katie's work. I was surrounded by young men and women who had just seen the play for the first time, and the energy was palpable. One of them had the courage to ask, "What makes something sexual assault?"

There it was. The reason we were all there. An environment had been carefully created that day by Katie and her colleagues, so that this young man felt not only safe enough to ask this question, but felt his responsibility to learn the answer to this question. You cannot fight what you do not know.

I have witnessed *Now That We're Men* become the first step in a long journey toward knowing that we have a problem. Knowing that the way we're teaching boys to be "men" is fundamentally broken. With the acknowledgment of that problem comes another step, one toward imagining a solution. As first steps go, this one is huge. A leap. Not of faith—nothing as enigmatic as that— but of clarity and urgency. A leap made with the knowledge that wherever you may land and no matter how hard it was to actually get there, it is worth it.

When you get there, you will be able to add yourself to this exhausting fight, this sometimes-thankless job of pushing back against oppression. You will realize, as I am beginning to, that what you are fighting is not so solid. These brutal systems are cracking and crumbling faster and faster because of the work *you* are doing—and because of the work of the brave ones who came before you.

Now That We're Men has already played a crucial role in creating some of the fighters that do this work. Katie Cappiello continues to play a crucial role in the creation of these fighters. This play will make you want to change the world. That will be your first step.

What will be your next?

Being an "angry young man" is both a cliché and a command. Even young boys are encouraged to channel any vulnerability into rage. Aggression is the one acceptable masculine way of expression.

Real Men: Introduction

Dominic Fumusa

In my early days in New York theater, I knew an actor who dealt with his nerves at auditions by getting really angry. The nervous part I understood, of course, but his rage response interested and perplexed me. Was this some macho version of imagining the audience naked? It seemed misguided.

One day, I asked this actor why auditions made him so angry. He said he didn't like handing over the power to his auditors. I didn't either, but I wondered, what would he do if the character he was auditioning for was supposed to be *happy*, or at least chill? This guy said that then he'd *have* to make the character angry. That's why he never went to auditions for television commercials; those characters are never angry. What would be the point? "Buy it! Or else!" Can you imagine?

A piece of me thought, *Good for him*. I mean, he may never work, he could end up starving to death, but damn it, he knew who he was as an artist and he wasn't going to betray that! This particular actor's rigid approach is not what they teach in theater—we train to be malleable—but that rigid approach *is* how a kid is usually taught to be a man. Being an "angry young man" is both a cliché and a command. Even young boys are encouraged to channel any vulnerability into rage. Aggression is the one acceptable masculine way of expression.

Even before I discovered that I loved theater—its immediacy, intimacy, and emotionality—I was a kid in Wisconsin, and I played football. I was quarterback from seventh grade through my junior year of college. The motivational power of rage was as much a part of my daily conditioning as isolation drills or yellow Gatorade. From a young age, I hung out with a "macho" set—athletes who easily got all of the attention at school and in our small town, even if they were dicks.

Later, I attended a small liberal arts college (Lawrence, in Appleton, Wisconsin), where I continued to do theater and play football (and majored in Government). I also joined a fraternity—the one with the biggest guys and loudest voices, though most of the frats were equally full of macho bullshit. I'm not proud of being part of the Greek system, but I know the frat world well. Looking back, I can see how fortunate I was that I had theater in my life. From age thirteen to twenty, football practice was followed by a quick dinner, and then I'd race to my rehearsal for the fall play. Always.

Shuttling back and forth between the two worlds gave me a little more space to be myself, in spite of how young men are socialized to turn away from emotion, openness, or softness. I quickly learned I couldn't be happy without making theater. And I learned how to take my aggression—from the football field and from those many messages about masculinity—and put it into my acting. It's true that, back then, I was drawn to the more . . . let's call it *butch* . . . version of being an actor. I *loved* the macho playwrights. I slept with a copy of Osborne's *Look Back in Anger* under my pillow. Shepard and Mamet were talking directly to me. My goal was to out-Brando Brando.

Of course, Mamet-loving or not, I was a football player who wanted to be an actor. I was called all the names. The football team could be relentless. In college, some of my teammates (who were also my fraternity brothers) came to see me in Ionesco's *Rhinoceros*. Afterwards, backstage, one of them said to me, "That was *really* good." I was thrilled—maybe he saw what was so powerful about theater! But then he followed that comment with, "It almost made up for the fact that I had to miss *MacGyver* tonight." I wanted to say, "Listen, you dummy. Live theater could make you a better person. You have a chance to connect—to yourself!—not sit in front of a TV and talk shit about women." But I didn't say that. I just laughed.

What I wish I'd have said to him is that a brilliant live performance is thrilling—as gripping as a goal-line stand with time running out. My first experience with *Now That We're Men* was a live performance by the original, brilliant cast, and it was *so fucking thrilling*. Picture five guys by turns razzing and being loyal to each other—puppyish and totally charming, even as they said the most disgusting things about sex and girls. In the ensemble scenes, these five characters are trying on manhood, but, in the heart-piercing monologues (which Katie calls "Confessionals"), they confide their interior lives. *That's* where we find the boys inside. We glimpse shame and insecurity in many varieties, about penis size, sexual abilities, sexuality, the inability to be a better man than one's asshole dad, and playing along with homophobic slurs. We perceive how much these young men need love and acceptance. We witness how exhausting it is to be essentially acting *all of the time*—but not in a theater, in daily *life*.

The show took my breath away and left me changed. The actors, actual teenagers and students of Katie's, were at ease with each other, as well as with this really difficult material. I was in awe of their commitment and courage. And then—and this is the transformative part—the courage was somehow extended to the audience. *I* felt brave getting to bear witness to them diving in, getting really messy. I got to retrieve (and forgive) a bit of my boyhood self. That's how generous this play is.

Whatever fear these young men felt about dramatizing elements of their real lives (and surely, given the content, they had a considerable amount of fear), it didn't prevent them from sharing their work with their fellow actors, and in turn, eventually, with you and me. Art is risky. In my opinion, no art form is riskier, more immediate, or better at getting at the truth than the theater. Truth-telling comes at a cost, but the cost of not doing it is much higher.

It's poignant to imagine what it would have meant to me as a kid in the 1980s to perform *Now That We're Men*. This play says what I didn't have language for as I was learning how to be a man. In fact, it says more about masculinity and male experience than most plays I've ever read. *Now That We're Men* allows me to see clearly that even as a straight, six-foot-two, football-playing frat brother, I was like the character of Andrew. I often felt like I was in a "fake-it-till-you-make-it situation," getting by until I could get away. Unlike Andrew, I could "prove" my "manliness" on the field; feeling I had to meant that I was scared of being seen as anything other than masculine. The get-out-of-jail-free card that was being a football player was bullshit. I knew this even back then, but I didn't always say so.

Those experiences, and my abashment about them, might be why, when I was just starting my career in New York (back when I was getting so angry at auditions—oh shit, did I just write that?), I was so grateful to appear in *Tape*. Stephen Belber wrote *Tape* for me and our mutual friend Josh Stamberg in 1999. Like *Now That We're Men*, *Tape* frames rape culture—in this case, the 1980s bros, beer, and blackouts version referenced at the confirmation hearings for Justice Kavanaugh—through the words and actions of guys. My character, Vince, a drug dealer, clandestinely records his friend, Jon (now a filmmaker), as they smoke pot and discuss whether or not Jon "date-raped" their friend, Amy, back in high school ten years earlier. We used the expression "date rape" back then, as if the act of rape was somehow less disgusting or less criminal if it occurred while out on a date or among "friends." Jon confesses, and Vince threatens to share the tape he's made with Amy, who is now an assistant DA.

By the way, it's an audio cassette tape! Do kids today even know what that is? I made the tape in a boom box! It all seems so quaint by today's standards. There was no uploading and downloading, no Snapchatting, Instagramming, or tweeting. Vince did not have the option of sharing with the whole world what Jon had or had not done to Amy. (In fact, Vince could barely make the tape, he was so stoned.) Today, as is expertly evoked in the action and set design of *Now That We're Men*, everything kids do seems to be recorded on their phones and posted for all the world to see—for eternity. This new reality (of unreality?) makes the characters of *Now That We're Men* more vulnerable—to harming themselves and others— than the characters in *Tape*.

The social-media-obsessed world the characters of Andrew, Derek, Evan, Marcus, and Nick have inherited accelerates a precarious, exciting, and promising time in their lives: the beginning, when they are all just starting to write their own stories. How can we support them to become the best possible men—the best possible human beings—they can be? *Now That We're Men*, the play and essays by real young people in this book, is a good place to start. Katie's empathy for how boys become men ignites conversations we too often avoid—to everyone's peril. *Now That We're Men* inspires me to cut through my own denial as a parent and encourages me to be honest with my fifteen-year-old daughter and twelve-year-old son about the pressures and messages I struggled with—and to listen to them, too.

The job of theater is literally catharsis—a safe purging of the toxic, scary, or shameful feelings we humans carry around with us, tucked into small pockets of our most hidden selves. Great playwrights write plays that scare us. They might create scenes, unfolding live before our very eyes, that feel so real that we, the audience, can hardly stand it. These are plays that make us feel things, uncomfortable things. That shake us. We might want to turn away, in fact, or flee. In a theater, we can look down at our program or close our eyes, but we can't change the channel or minimize the screen or press mute. We sit with the hard feelings and, in bearing witness together, we are changed—at least a bit, and maybe a whole lot.

I know I'm transformed because of *Now That We're Men*. I'm grateful for the reminder that theater can still save guys from the rage-filled "performance" of being a man and offer a path to being real.

Cast

Now That We're Men, by Katie Cappiello, with sound and projection design by Daniel Melnick, lighting design and stage management by Lauren Bremen, and directed by Katie Cappiello, had its premiere performance on February 6, 2016, at Dixon Place, NYC, with the following cast:

CAST
(In order of appearance)

MARCUS	Caleb Grandoit
NICK	Fred Hechinger
DEREK	Rayshawn Richardson
EVAN	Alphonso Jones
ANDREW	Jordan Eliot

Characters

MARCUS: High school junior, 17.

NICK: High school junior, 17.

DEREK: High school junior, 16.

EVAN: High school junior, 17.

ANDREW: High school junior, 16.

Time
Early March, present day.

Place
New York City.

NOTE: This play was conceived with a goal of creating substantial roles for men of color. Thus, in the original cast, MARCUS, DEREK, and EVAN were played by African American actors, as the parts clearly call for. The roles of NICK and ANDREW can be played by actors of any race.

SCENE 1. WILL SHE SAY YES?

SCENE: MARCUS, NICK, EVAN, DEREK, and ANDREW *hang out in the back of their school auditorium around a central bench with some chairs, school backpacks, and a bouquet of garish, cheap flowers. As the lights fade, they come to a freeze. The only light source now comes from a video projection of a school hallway hitting the center screen, a text conversation between* MARCUS *and his mom:*

MARCUS. *Am i gonna look like a fool if i do this?*

MOM. *No!!*

MARCUS. *I'd rather die than look like a fool in front of everyone*

MOM. *Ahhh be a man baby boy. Do your thang!! She's gonna love it*

A school bell rings. Lights up, the boys stand in formation and "You're All I Need to Get By" by Marvin Gaye begins to play. They rehearse full-out an elaborate,

*choreographed dance and lip-synched
routine, all part of* MARCUS*'s "promposal"
plan.*

MARCUS. Sara . . . *(very dramatic)* all I
need is for you to say yes to this: Will
you go to prom with me? *(To* NICK*)* Yo,
now's when you hand me the flowers.
*(*NICK *passes him the flowers.)* Then we
wait for her to say yes and then we're
all good. What do you think?

NICK. I think she's gonna say yes.

EVAN. Dude, come on, you know she's
gonna say yes.

DEREK. She might not.

MARCUS. What, son?!

DEREK. Man, I got your back and all on
this, but it's kinda cheesy.

ANDREW. No!

DEREK. Uh, yes. It is. You should just
bring her flowers and be subtle—this
is too over the top.

NICK. No it's good, you're wrong. I did
that cupcake thing—I spelled it out
in cupcakes for Rebecca—she really
loved it. Everyone was talking about
it, and—

MARCUS. Exactly. And yo, did you check
those YouTube videos I sent you? It's,

like, it's cheesy but also hilarious and also, like . . . you're the man if you're willing to make an ass of yourself for a girl.

ANDREW. True.

EVAN. Definitely—but only if you're already on top, you know?

ANDREW. What?

EVAN. I'm saying you can't be, like, Theo Sanders or, like, Randolf Cummings or a kid like that and do this shit. You already have to have some clout. Otherwise you're just fucking lame as fuck.

ANDREW. So, wait, can we go over the plan again?

MARCUS. Yeah, so tomorrow, I'm just gonna be real distant to her all day so she doesn't suspect anything, and then, you guys need to be spread out throughout the cafeteria so when it starts it feels like a flash mob.

NICK. But this isn't really a flash mob.

MARCUS. It kind of is because we're, like, mobbing her out of nowhere with this routine—

NICK. No. A flash mob is really, like, when people add on and there's, like, more than fucking five people.

EVAN. Dude, will you shut the fuck up so he can tell us the plan and we can go. I got band practice.

DEREK. Band nerd! The band nerd's gotta hurry so he can start blowing his clarinet, everyone!

EVAN. Keep talking, asshole. For real, keep talking. When I get a scholarship to fucking Howard or some shit because of my clarinet, you can suck my dick, how's that?

ANDREW. Can you guys shut up? Okay, so we're spread out. Nick has the flowers. Who's gonna have the speakers?

DEREK. I am.

MARCUS. Yo, you're not gonna fuck this up, right?

DEREK. Please.

MARCUS. No, for real. This has to be perfect. I like . . . I don't know. Sara, man . . .

ANDREW. He loves her.

MARCUS. Shut the fuck up.

ANDREW. You do. Look at you!

MARCUS. Real quick, Derek. Show me the step-snap stuff again.

DEREK. No. I got it.

MARCUS. Andrew, show him. (ANDREW

shows DEREK. MARCUS *to* DEREK.) Get it on your phone. Seriously, yo! Get your phone out and record it so you can practice—because you're not gonna make me look bad.

EVAN. You know, my mom and dad, they went to prom together.

NICK. What do you mean?

EVAN. That was, like, their first official date.

MARCUS. Oh yeah?!

EVAN. Yeah.

NICK. That's awesome. I would so marry Rebecca. Like, if we stay in touch when we're in our thirties. I'll be making movies, right? She'll be, like, some like—

ANDREW. A writer, I think. She's gonna write novels or something, right?

MARCUS. So, did your dad tap that ass?

DEREK. Yo!!!

MARCUS. Did he?

DEREK. Do you gotta talk about his parents fucking, man?

EVAN. I have no idea. You think I asked him that?! I doubt it. My mom wasn't like that.

MARCUS. Like what?

ANDREW. His mom wasn't a slut is what he's saying.

DEREK. Well, Marcus, you're good, bro. Sara's pretty thotty. You're gonna get yours at after-prom.

ANDREW. She's not thotty.

MARCUS, EVAN, NICK, DEREK. Yeah she is.

EVAN. But I don't think she's gonna fuck you.

MARCUS. What are you talking about, son? If she says yes it's kinda implied.

EVAN, NICK, ANDREW. No.

MARCUS. Please.

EVAN. She's thotty but she doesn't actually have sex with lots of people.

ANDREW. Then what makes her thotty?

EVAN. I don't know—

DEREK. She blew that freshman at Sean's party last weekend. She's always got her tits out.

EVAN. Yeah.

ANDREW. Who gives a shit? And you let a girl blow you at Sean's last weekend even though you're talking to Kelsey— you're thotty. Plus you like her tits.

DEREK. I really do.

MARCUS. Me too.

NICK. She is kinda slutty, dude. Sorry. I love Sara—she's our friend—

EVAN. We're all friends with her—we're not saying we don't like her—

NICK. Yeah, and she's so nice and shit, but she's always up on everybody.

MARCUS. Exactly, and I'm gonna get her!

EVAN. I don't think so, man, no.

ANDREW. I agree.

MARCUS. I'll fucking bet you guys!

EVAN. Oh, come on.

MARCUS. What? Be men now . . . come on.

EVAN. Yo, *you* be a man and try to get yours if you want. It's not about us.

MARCUS. Don't be pussies—bet me!

ANDREW. Fine. I'll bet you she doesn't sleep with you. What are we betting?

MARCUS. Hundred bucks. Each.

EVAN. You don't have two hundred bucks.

MARCUS. Fuck you. I do.

EVAN. Fine, a hundred bucks each says she does not fuck you. FUCK. Not blow you or whack you off, FUCK you.

MARCUS. Yo, I feel bad for you because you both just lost a hundred bucks, bitches.

EVAN. Okay!

ANDREW. Dude, you were just talking about how much you like this girl. We're doing this idiotic thing for her and you're talking shit.

MARCUS. I'm not talking shit, but you guys are basically saying I'm not a man and I can't bang this girl.

EVAN. Pretty much.

NICK. Well, she's gotta say yes to prom first.

MARCUS. She will.

NICK. Should we practice again?

DEREK. I can't. I'm hungry—I need snacks, I gotta go.

EVAN. Me too, band, man.

MARCUS. Okay. Yo, please promise me you're gonna practice. All of you. For real?

NICK. We will. Later, man. *(*EVAN, NICK, DEREK *exit.)*

MARCUS. What do you think?

ANDREW. It's gonna be good.

MARCUS. Yeah. I like her so fucking much!

ANDREW *and* MARCUS *laugh and further plan as they grab their bags and start exiting the stage. Meanwhile,* EVAN *reenters as the focus shifts to him. The house lights come up and he addresses the audience directly, even walking into the audience at times.*

CONFESSIONAL: EVAN

EVAN. I'm good now. I wasn't for a while, but . . . I'm straightening out and trying to get my shit together. My friends were like, why'd you miss school?—I missed a band competition, too—and I told 'em I had, like, a bad case of strep, you know? Because . . . I don't know . . . I'm not about to share one of my weaker moments with them. Please. In order to graduate you have to pass swimming. You take it at school and everyone puts on the school bathing suits and you do laps and prove you can swim. After swimming this one time, I was in the locker room, and I'm trying to change into my clothes—and I hate the locker room. Everyone acts like a fucking dick in there, man. More so than anywhere else, in my opinion. Someone's always gotta be acting big, whipping someone with a wet towel, and the guys who are jacked up are always acting like

they're ready to fucking throw down,
like, right there, near the showers,
you know? Whatever. So I'm trying
to change and this dude just grabs
my towel and yanks it off. And I'm
standing there. And all these guys
are looking at me. And this dude
Raymond, who everyone thinks is
the fucking man—you know—he's
always giving daps, being an asshole,
roughing people up, talking shit
about girls, right? He's that guy in
the hallway, you know. He goes, "Yo,
look at Little Dick!" And that was it.
And I'm trying to get my clothes and
all these guys are fucking dying being
like, "Little Dick, hey, Little Dick,
what can you fuck with that little dick,
man?" And it's just going on and on.
Listen, I am a black man, okay? And
as a black man, this is not something
I want to hear—it's not supposed to be
my reality, you know what I'm saying?
I've got these, like, five-foot-three little
white dudes in my gym class calling
me "Little Dick"? Fuck that. I was,
like, crashing, man. I felt pretty much
destroyed . . . for real. Like no doubt
in my mind that this shit was gonna
get around. So I got home and I was
just distraught. I think I was having a

panic attack when I think back about it. My older brother, JR, he still lives at home, and we share a room and he was like, "Yo, what's your deal man?" And I told him, which was a mistake. *(Beat.)* He thought it was fucking hilarious. And he told my dad. And that . . . man . . . *(Beat.)* And my dad . . . my dad whooped my ass. Hard. And he was like, "Be a man—men don't let people talk down to them like that. You let those kids belittle you and you did nothing? What's wrong with you? Man up. You hear me?" And he's like spitting in my face and he's like, "You need to learn to man the fuck up." Actually, he didn't say *fuck*. My dad doesn't curse. So . . . whatever. And I was just feeling bad. I don't know how to explain it. It was bad in that moment. It's like, I don't play sports, okay? I don't kick it to, like, lots of girls usually, I don't fight people, and my dad thinks I'm a fucking pussy . . . I don't know. But I was, like, on the ground that night. I've never felt like that before. And I just went into the bathroom and took a shitload of pills. Like anything I could get my hands on: ibuprofen, Sudafed, Benadryl, aspirin, my brother's Ritalin

. . . handfuls of pills. And I passed out. That's all I remember. I woke up in the hospital. They pumped my stomach. My parents were worried but pissed. I would never tell anybody about that. No. I'm actually fucking ashamed of that day. Putting my parents through that. And I wasn't really trying to kill myself. Please. I was just losing it is all. I think I was kind of acting like a scared little kid that day. *(Beat.)* And I don't like what my dad did, but he was looking out. That's all. When you're a man you gotta get respect, and I was not respected that day in the locker room, and I'm not having that, you know? I'm not riding that train. I'm gonna get mine—you know?

SCENE 2. YOUR SISTER'S TITS

SCENE: *House lights fade and the only light comes from the projections on the screen. A video of a subway train rushing through the station is projected and loud subway sounds roar as we see a text conversation between* NICK *and his mom:*

MOM. *Don't forget—tutor coming at 5pm!*

NICK. *Bout to get on train should be there right on time*

Lights come up as NICK *and* ANDREW *enter with their backpacks, hustling onto a crowded 4 or 5 train—the central bench serves as the subway seats.*

NICK. Yo, get those seats—those—

ANDREW. Can you move that way? *(They settle in but they are packed tight)* Okay . . . keep going—

NICK. Right. So, she's talking to Ava about the whole Jack thing.

ANDREW. What Jack thing?

NICK. I don't even really know, some bullshit about Jack being a douchebag or whatever, it's really not the point.

ANDREW. Okay, yeah.

NICK. And she goes to Ava—like right in front of me—"Nick's not the hot guy type, so I don't get what you're going through."

ANDREW. What?!

NICK. Yeah, fucking yes, that's what she said. *(ANDREW is laughing hysterically.)* Dude, it's not funny.

ANDREW. Yes, it is.

NICK. But wait though, 'cause then Ava says to Rebecca, "True—you've got a Chandler."

ANDREW. Wait—Chandler from *Friends*?

NICK. Yeah. *(ANDREW is laughing hysterically now.)* And I really can't stand that show—it's lowbrow and the characters all are one-dimensional privileged white people with—

ANDREW. Could you *BE* any more Chandler?!

NICK. Fuck you, man. *(ANDREW tries to regain control.)* What does she mean by that? That I'm not, I don't know, is she saying I'm not good-looking?

ANDREW. No.

NICK. But that's basically what she said.

ANDREW. No, she was saying you're not a dick.

NICK. Then why would she say the "not the hot guy type" thing?

ANDREW. I don't know—'cause guys who look like Jack are assholes.

NICK. Right, but that's saying I'm not hot or whatever, not that I really care, but she's saying she doesn't consider me hot.

ANDREW. Obviously you're "hot" to *her*— she's getting with you, isn't she?

NICK. But, so, then, I'm not hot to other people? I'm not generally good-looking then—?

ANDREW. Yeah, I don't know.

NICK. What's bad about the way I look?

ANDREW. This is fucking stupid—nothing! I don't know.

NICK. It's annoying. I feel kinda shitty about this. I shouldn't. I mean, fuck her.

ANDREW. Yeah, stop.

NICK. Like, what's wrong with you that you'd go and say something like that about a guy you're supposed to like, you know? It's cunty.

ANDREW. *(Noticing someone down at the far end of the subway car.)* Hey—

NICK. Man, I *never* walk around and think, "Oh, fuck, I'm not good-looking, what am I gonna do," or whatever, but now I'm thinking about it.

ANDREW. Hey—

NICK. Like, what? Do I need to work out now? Should I be working out? She sucks.

ANDREW. Ted Wayland.

NICK. What?

ANDREW. Ted's on this train.

NICK. Where?

ANDREW. Down there.

NICK. Oh yeah. I see him. *(Silence.)*

NICK. Anyway . . . I don't know about Rebecca.

ANDREW. Why do people like that kid?

NICK. I know.

ANDREW. Yeah, but you hang out with him.

NICK. Not really—

ANDREW. Okay.

NICK. We're not friends—I mean, I've spoken to him before at parties and stuff, so have you. It's not like he comes to my house.

ANDREW. Yeah.

NICK. But I agree with you. The kid's a dick.

ANDREW. He's a bad fucking person. *(Silence.)* I kinda want to do something.

NICK. What do you mean?

ANDREW. I want to go up to him and say something.

NICK. I wouldn't do that.

ANDREW. Why?

NICK. Because you're gonna make it a bigger thing.

ANDREW. He made it a big thing when he passed that shit around.

NICK. I know. But you're not gonna go over there and get in his face on this train, come on.

ANDREW. I wanna be like, "What you did was fucked up. Did you think for a fucking second what it was going to do to her?"

NICK. Obviously not.

ANDREW. I don't know. I think—

NICK. He didn't, man, come on. Are you telling me when he sent that around he meant to mess with her? No.

ANDREW. Okay, then he just wasn't thinking of her—that's good, that's better.

NICK. That's not what I'm saying.

ANDREW. *(Feeling claustrophobic.)* Do you have any room?

NICK. No, dude. And can you stop pushing—

ANDREW. It's really fucking hot on this train.

NICK. I know, but you're making it worse when you—

ANDREW. Look at him. Who's he with? I can't see.

NICK. Lauren Horowitz and Dan.

ANDREW. Lauren?! Are you serious?

NICK. What?

ANDREW. If Elizabeth saw that, she'd kill herself. For real.

NICK. Oh, come on.

ANDREW. What? Lauren is one of her best friends and now she's hanging out with Ted—

NICK. Maybe she doesn't know about the pictures.

ANDREW. She knows. My sister can't talk about anything else right now. So there is no way Lauren doesn't know.

NICK. Maybe she doesn't think it's as big a deal as Elizabeth does?

ANDREW. Really? Well if Ted shared a nude of Lauren with, like, half the fucking guys—

NICK. It's not like Elizabeth's is the only picture out there.

ANDREW. What?

NICK. I'm just saying she's not the only one—

ANDREW. Yeah well, she's my sister—

NICK. I know but—

ANDREW. Guys I know are jerking off to my sister! You know?

NICK. Well . . . maybe not.

ANDREW. What?

NICK. They might not be, is all I'm saying.

ANDREW. I don't get that—you're saying they're maybe not jerking off to the shit on their phones or they're maybe not jerking off to her?

NICK. Aah—I don't know, man—I don't know—I don't really want to talk to you about your sister and her tits, okay?

ANDREW. Well, it sounds like you're talking shit about Liz and saying her body's, like, not worthy of a whack-off!

NICK. Okay, hey, man, I'm sorry but this is just really weird now. *(Silence. Then he takes out his phone.)* But, lemme ask you this, what are *you* doing with *this*?

ANDREW. What?

NICK. Or this one?

ANDREW. You're gonna pull those up on the train? People can see those.

NICK. No.

ANDREW. Oh, they can't see what's on your phone? When you're in public and they're, like, hovering over us?

NICK. Fine, but I sent those to you after Abby and Fiona sent them to me and you weren't concerned about it. Were you? *(Beat.)* Did you jerk off to these?

ANDREW. No.

NICK. Lie.

ANDREW. Nick, I see Abby and Fiona every day, I can jerk off to them without seeing their naked asses if I really want to.

NICK. But you looked at the pics.

ANDREW. You sent them to me!

NICK. I did. And it was no big deal. Do you think they're scarred because you've seen their asses?

ANDREW. Possibly.

NICK. No way.

ANDREW. Liz is scarred.

NICK. Only because she found out. And I don't know whose fault that is. Who told her? Lauren? Jessie? Well, they should've kept their mouths shut.

ANDREW. That was never gonna happen.

NICK. Well, Abby and Fiona don't know you've seen those pics, so they're not damaged by it.

ANDREW. Ridiculous . . . seriously though, why did you send me those?

NICK. They're funny. I wanted to you to see. These girls are crazy, man—Fiona's ass. Fucking insane.

ANDREW. Fucked up.

NICK. Okay, well, why didn't you call me out before then? You're all preaching about it now, you're offended now—by Ted and apparently by me too—so what? Now that it's Lizzy it's ethically fucked up? I think that's strange, man. It's hypocritical.

ANDREW. Look at him. He's such a piece of shit. Always wearing that Tufts sweatshirt. He doesn't go there. Who does he even know that goes there, for real? He's such—

NICK. Okay, what about Jennifer Lawrence?

ANDREW. What about her?

NICK. We looked at those. Was that wrong?

ANDREW. She's a celebrity.

NICK. So.

ANDREW. It's different.

NICK. Not really.

ANDREW. Dude, she's not a minor. So yeah, it's different. And she's a public figure and she's not, like, going to school every day, seeing people every day in classes who have seen her naked body. It's really fucking different, okay? I'm gonna say something to him. I'm just gonna get off when he gets off and say something. He's gotta bc called out on this shit and Elizabeth won't do it. She sent him a text that was like, "You're so wrong," but she's not gonna actually confront him—

NICK. I really think you need to not do that.

ANDREW. Well, you don't have a sister—you don't get it. Liz is ready to like slit her wrists because that fucker pulled up a picture of my sister's naked body and sent it to every kid on the hockey team and they sent it to a whole shitload of other people.

NICK. Come on, man. It wasn't even her whole body.

ANDREW. What are you talking about?

NICK. It was just a tit pic, man. Eighth grade shit.

ANDREW. You saw it?

NICK. What do you mean?

ANDREW. You saw the picture of Liz?

NICK. Well, yeah.

ANDREW. How?

NICK. Someone sent it to me.

ANDREW. Who?

NICK. Why does it matter?

ANDREW. I wanna know.

NICK. Evan.

ANDREW. What?!

NICK. Yeah.

ANDREW. Who sent it to him?

NICK. I don't know, man. It's just making the rounds, you know?

ANDREW. How can you say that so casually?

NICK. Because it is casual!

ANDREW. It's not.

NICK. Man, *she* sent it to *him*!

ANDREW. Meaning what?

NICK. Meaning your sister that you're so worried about took off her fucking shirt and took a pic, and then *she* sent it to *Ted*. She knew what she was doing, man.

ANDREW. She didn't know he would share it with, like, the world.

NICK. How could she not have known that?

ANDREW. I one hundred percent do not think she knew he was gonna do that.

NICK. Okay, well, ignorance isn't an excuse.

ANDREW. What?!

NICK. Just 'cause she may claim she didn't know what he would do—which I still don't believe—doesn't mean she's exempt from the reality . . . the consequences or whatever. She sent something to him. Then it became his. And he did what he wanted with it. She put it out there. She made a choice.

ANDREW. She Snapchatted it!

NICK. Right, and he took a screenshot. Sorry. She knows people do that.

ANDREW. Why is it on her?!

NICK. Because she made the initial move. She wanted Ted to pay attention to her so she—*(ANDREW grabs him.)*

ANDREW. Shut the fuck up.

NICK. Yo! *(Trying to push ANDREW off of him and looking around at his fellow riders.)*

ANDREW. He's the one who did the fucked up thing, though. *(Really up in his face and shaking him.)*

NICK. Dude, stop, we're on the train.

ANDREW. I don't give a fuck.

NICK. Come on, you're embarrassing yourself—

ANDREW. You have her picture on your phone right now?

NICK. Seriously, stop grabbing me like this—

ANDREW. Do you?

NICK. Yes.

ANDREW. You're a fucking bad friend. Delete it now.

NICK. Okay.

ANDREW. I'm serious. Delete it now.

NICK. Okay, let go of me and I'll do it.

(ANDREW lets go of NICK and NICK deletes

it. Silence. The people around them are staring at them. Beat.)

ANDREW. She took the picture. And she sent it to him. Fine. He just clearly has, like, no respect for her at all to send it around like that. She didn't give him permission to share it. And I get that it's what people do. I've done it too. But it's like . . . you don't live with her, man.

NICK. Yeah.

ANDREW. You don't see how bad she feels. She really seriously did not think he was gonna do that. And we're assholes for doing that shit, too. 'Cause if you saw her at home—you'd be like, I don't know, you'd be like, "It can't be right if this girl is this messed up about it."

NICK. Do your parents know?

ANDREW. No.

NICK. She gonna tell them?

ANDREW. No. They'd be pissed at her for sending it.

NICK. Yeah.

ANDREW. This ride is taking forever.

NICK. So what do you think I should do about Rebecca?

ANDREW. I don't really give a fuck, honestly.

NICK. Yeah. It's just that it's embarrassing that she said that. You think she's saying it to other people too?

(We hear the muffled announcement, "This is 14th Street Union Square. Transfer is available to . . .")

ANDREW. He's getting off!

NICK. What?

ANDREW. Ted. He's getting off. I'm getting off!

NICK. Seriously?

ANDREW. Yeah. I gotta do it. *(To the people on the train.)* Excuse me. I'm getting off. *(To* NICK.*)* You coming?

NICK. Uh . . . nah. I gotta get home.

ANDREW. Fine. (ANDREW *exits. After a second,* NICK *tries to exit too. But it's too late. We hear "Stand clear of the closing doors please . . ." and the accompanying bing-bing of the door closing.)*

NICK. Too late. Fuck.

(Nowhere for him to sit, NICK *stands as the train heads to the next stop.)*

MARCUS *enters. House lights up.* MARCUS *directs his confessional to the audience.*

CONFESSIONAL: MARCUS

MARCUS. She was late, you know? She texted me, and she was like, "I missed my period." And I was like, "What the fuck?" I mean, I was pissed. I, like, pretty much lost my shit with her: "You said you were on the pill, what the fuck were you thinking?" And she's coming back at me like, "What are we gonna do? Are you gonna man up and be a father to this kid?" And I just ghosted. I went dark. She kept texting and calling and I was just like, nah. I didn't want to deal with it. (NICK *gets off subway car and exits.*) She's not pregnant anymore. I know that. She had a miscarriage or whatever. I think God was looking out for me there, because that girl would have hunted me down for money, no doubt. Money I don't fucking have. Same kinda money my mother never got from my father, you know? I was about to be part of that circle of bullshit. And now, I'm not—because God wanted a different path for me. I really believe that. And maybe that sounds fucked up, but . . . it is what it is. That's the truth for me. My boys don't know. And, um, my mother has no idea. And it makes me sick thinking of how bad it would have been to tell my mom I knocked some girl up. 'Cause my mom's everything to me, and she's done everything for me—she's up my ass, yeah, but she works like a fucking dog to keep things going for us. She had me when she was sixteen. And she's been doing it on her own. Which is whatever, you know? Is what it is. But I have this picture of the two of us in my room. It's taped to the wall. Like, an old-school photo. And it's my mom and me and she's seventeen in the picture, and I'm, like, one, and I'm screaming, trying to fly outta her arms, and she's laughing, trying to hold me, and she's looking into the camera. And she looks freaked the fuck out! *(He laughs.)* Like she's smiling—but she's scared, right? But I love the picture because it's so us, you know. And I'm looking at this picture last night and I'm like, she was a fucking kid with a kid. And my pops was like, "Peace. Fuck this bitch. She can deal with this baby." And I get that he was bugging out but . . . how did he do that to her? I fucking hate the dude. I don't even know him but I want to beat his ass like it's never been beat before. But I'm him, right? And I hate that. When my girl told me she was late, I was him. And I don't want to know that about myself, but *I do.* Come on, you know? I *DO*—I *know* that. And it would kill my mom if she knew how I treated that girl, right? And she's in my head, and balancing my mom and who my mom wants me to be, and the type of man I want to be for her, right? With the piece of shit I really am sometimes . . . I don't know. Makes me want to take a hit, man. (Derek *and* Evan *enter,* Evan *gets down to the floor center-stage and starts doing pushups as* Derek *watches him.*)

I'm telling you. Makes me want to roll a big ol' joint and just . . . *(He mimes taking a hit.)* 'Cause my mom's in my head all the time and I love her but I'm weaker than she would want me to be . . .

SCENE 3: DEEP THROAT

SCENE: *House lights fade on the scene and go to black; the only light comes from the projections on the screen. Video of the lights coming on in a big school gymnasium appears on the screen. We hear the sounds of loud, industrial switches being turned on as a text conversation between* EVAN *and his mom pops up:*

EVAN. *Killed the history test! Gonna workout w Derek and Marcus now*

MOM. *That's what I love to hear! Home by 7 please.*

Lights up and MARCUS *enters the scene.*

DEREK. You gotta touch your nose to the floor.

EVAN. Shut up.

DEREK. You do, yo, or you're not fully engaging the muscles.

MARCUS. *(Entering the scene.)* Tighten your core, man.

DEREK. It's like this. *(Shows him.)* All the way down. That's the only way you exhaust the muscles. Exhausting the muscles is the thing.

EVAN. Shut the fuck up.

DEREK. You're just half-assing it.

MARCUS. You're not gonna gain bulk like that, man.

EVAN. Who says I wanna gain bulk?

DEREK. Oh, okay. You just went to GNC and dropped your dog-walking money on like a gallon of protein powder—

MARCUS. But he's not trying to get big though!

DEREK. Right?! Please, bro.

MARCUS. We know you're trying to get rid of those chicken legs.

EVAN. Look who's fucking talking, man? *(His phone gets a notification.)*

MARCUS. Strong and lean. What are you doing this for anyway?

DEREK. He's got lots of band concerts coming up—he's gotta beef up so he can dominate that clarinet. *(He gets another notification.)*

MARCUS. Takes a lotta man power to hit those notes, right, son?

EVAN. Actually it does—but I'm glad to see you guys are powering up for all the hours you spend on your asses playing *GTA*. Gotta get those thumbs in shape, boys.

DEREK. Nah—I'm going out for basketball—

MARCUS. That's hilarious!

DEREK. Why you saying that?

MARCUS. 'Cause your skills are weak, kid! *(EVAN on his phone.)*

DEREK. Man, you wish you had my game.

MARCUS. I could be on the basketball team if I wanted to—some of us gotta work, rich boy.

DEREK. *(Laughs.)* I'm not rich.

MARCUS. You're richer than me, Richie Rich.

EVAN. *(Focused on his phone.)* And me.

DEREK. Why you gotta be saying that?

EVAN. Dude, your dad's a fucking lawyer.

DEREK. So.

MARCUS. "Kenneth Davis. Attorney at Law." Your pops is basically white, yo.

DEREK. What?

MARCUS. What?

DEREK. Man . . . see, that's the problem! That's how they're fucking with us, man. What you just said is fucked up.

MARCUS. How so?

DEREK. You are equating my dad being successful to him being white. By saying that you're saying only white people can be successful. That's racist. *(Another notification.)*

MARCUS. HA. Funny. See my skin, man? I'm a black man. Can't be racist against my own.

DEREK. And my dad is black, man. But, you think he's not black enough because he's a lawyer—and that's bullshit. Barack Obama is a lawyer.

EVAN. He's a little bit white, actually.

MARCUS. True.

DEREK. So, what's your dad do?

MARCUS. I have no idea. Don't know the dude.

DEREK. So is that "black" then? Is that "so black" of your life?

MARCUS. Now *that's* really fucking racist. *(*EVAN*'s phone.)*

DEREK. Yo! You're basically saying my dad's, like, a nerdy pussy white dude because he worked hard and now I don't have to have a job because he can give me an allowance and I can focus on school? And I'm racist? Nah. That's bullshit—I'm calling *you* out on *your* racist shit.

MARCUS. I'm just saying you kinda living a white life, is all. Don't be sad 'cause you're an Oreo, son.

DEREK. If I were an Oreo, would I be hanging out with you?

MARCUS. Definitely. Politically correct and shit. Just own it.

DEREK. Success shouldn't mean a white life—

MARCUS. But it does, white boy.

DEREK. Whatever, fucked up. *(Evan's phone.)* YO! Who the fuck is blowing up your fucking phone?

EVAN. What?

MARCUS. Your phone.

EVAN. Yeah.

DEREK. It's irritating the hell out of me. Can you turn the notification sounds off or something so we don't have to hear it every fucking time? Who is it?

EVAN. Sonia.

MARCUS. She dropping your ass yet?

EVAN. I don't know. There's, like, a thing going on—

DEREK. What thing?

EVAN. Nothing, just some bullshit.

DEREK. About what?

EVAN. Nothing.

MARCUS. Okay.

EVAN. She's being all intense about some shit that went down the other night, it's like—

DEREK. Awww . . . did you touch her titties and she didn't like it?

EVAN. Nah. It wasn't that. I mean, I did, but she liked that.

MARCUS. Nice! 'Bout fucking time. How long you've been working this girl, man? Like two months. Were you like, "I'm a man, bitch! I got needs, baby"?

EVAN. Uh, no. That's fucking ridiculous and I would never say that shit. *(Back to his phone.)*

DEREK. So what happened? You're messing around . . . finally . . . and what then? What's she all sensitive about?

EVAN. Fuck.

MARCUS. What?

EVAN. She's just really tight with me, man.

DEREK. For what?!

EVAN. I don't know—

MARCUS. Okay.

EVAN. I don't know what the deal is really. So, I don't know . . . last night, right? She's at my place.

MARCUS. Whoa, she went all the way out to Bay-fucking-Ridge?

DEREK. That's what's up.

MARCUS. Oh, like you get it, Manhattan boy.

DEREK. Man . . .

MARCUS. Were your parents out?

EVAN. Obviously. So we're watching *American Horror Story* or whatever and she's, like, lying on me, you know. And stuff starts to go down a little bit and I've got her shirt off and, like, I kinda can't believe it because it's going further than it ever has, right? So I'm like, "Let's go into the bedroom." And she gets shy about it, but then she's like, "Yeah okay." So we go into my room and we're doing a little of this and a little of that and then I told her, you know, I told her I wanted her to suck me off.

DEREK. Damn!

EVAN. Hold up, though. So I'm thinking, like, no way is she going to do it, but then she's on her fucking knees and I was like, "Oh shit."

MARCUS. OH SHIT! And she's such a good girl too.

DEREK. I like good girls.

MARCUS. Me too.

EVAN. Wait, okay. Just lemme—so she's doing it, and she's really into it, for real, and I'm into it too, obviously. And so she stops for a second to, like, come up for air or whatever, I have no idea.

MARCUS. Breathe through your nose, girl, come on.

DEREK. Man, she's a beginner. Cut her some slack.

EVAN. Yeah, I don't know. So, I don't know, then I was like . . . fuck, never mind, this is fucking stupid. It's fine, let's just—

DEREK. No, dude. What?

MARCUS. You're getting to the good stuff and you're cutting out? Nah. Go.

EVAN. *(He sighs and starts to laugh a little—it's kind of awkward.)* I said to her . . . I said, "Can I deep throat you?"

(MARCUS *and* DEREK *burst into laughter.*)

MARCUS. Okay!

DEREK. Wait. You actually, said it, like, out loud?

EVAN. Yeah.

(DEREK *and* MARCUS *find this hilarious. They are impressed; they are surprised. It's a good story.*)

DEREK. What did she say?

EVAN. So she goes, like, totally relaxed, like, she wasn't pissed that I asked at all, she just goes, "Um, I don't really want to do that, if that's okay? I don't like it."

MARCUS. Not her first time apparently!

EVAN. She's like, "I'm down to do keep doing it but I just don't want to do that."

MARCUS. Hey, whatever. Always next time, right?

EVAN. Yeah . . . yeah. So, whatever, she gets back to it and I've got my hands on her head . . . 'cause, like, where else do you put them, right?

DEREK. On your hips, man. Superman that shit!

MARCUS. How 'bout behind your head—
just chillin'? *(They laugh.)*

EVAN. No, no, no—seriously. Come on—
lemme just finish the story—

DEREK. Sorry, man, we're playing, we're
playing! Okay, so . . .

EVAN. And I'm into it and I don't know, I
kind of just, I don't even really know
what happened, but, like, I was just
really into it and I pulled on her head
and, like, sort of, like, pushed myself
further down her throat.

MARCUS. What'd she do?

EVAN. I mean, I don't know—I think it
kind of freaked her out because she
grabbed on to my legs and then she
sort of started pushing my legs a little
and she was moaning—and I, at first I
was like, "Oh, she's liking this," right?
But then I felt her . . . gag or whatever
. . . and so I let go of her head and . . .
like . . . she . . . she threw up. And she
was coughing and stuff.

DEREK. That's fucking disgusting.

EVAN. I mean, she cried and shit.

DEREK. She cried?

EVAN. Yeah.

DEREK. Why?

MARCUS. 'Cause the dude choked her.

EVAN. Yo, I didn't mean . . .

MARCUS. You did, though. You choked your girl, man.

EVAN. It wasn't like that.

MARCUS. Wasn't like what?

EVAN. I don't know . . . I was just in the moment! And . . . I don't know, but she got all pissed. And she was like, "I can't believe you just did that to me." And she goes, "You really hurt me." And I was like . . . *(remembering what he said to her)* . . . fuck, I really shouldn't have said this now that I think about it. . . . Fucking stupid, but I said, "Yeah, I guess I got carried away. I didn't mean for it to hurt you. It's just that it's a turn-on to do it but I shouldn't have done it to you." *(Silence.)*

DEREK. What'd she say?

EVAN. She was just, like, crying, and I mean, there was throw-up on my floor that I had to clean up. It was fucking gross. And she got her bag and stuff and was like, "Fuck you," and just, like, left. *(Silence.)* Then, like, late last night I get this text from her and she's like *(reading the text)*, "I need you to know what you did was not okay. I told you I didn't want to do something and you did it. You basically assaulted me and words can't describe how upset I am and how violated I feel."

DEREK. She used the word "violated"? Oh my god, man, that's like a serious overreaction.

MARCUS. You think so?

DEREK. Yeah. I mean, he didn't violate her, man. What the fuck? Things were going down and he got too excited and he got a little, I don't know, aggressive maybe—if that's fucking assault now, then we're all fucked. The girl was on her knees, man. Come on, she was down for it. That's ridiculous.

MARCUS. Yeah? Interesting.

EVAN. So I've been texting with her all last night and today. She's not going to prom with me anymore now.

DEREK. Are you serious?

EVAN. Yeah, and I called and left her this voicemail and shit. I mean, I feel fucking bad that she's so upset. I was like, "I'm sorry you're upset. I'm sorry you feel like I violated you. I guess I just went too far, you know? I think we should still do prom—" All that type of shit. And, "I never meant to hurt you and I definitely don't want you to feel like I assaulted you—it wasn't assault, it was just something that got out of control."

MARCUS. You said that?

EVAN. Basically. And I was like, "I hope you know I really respect you and I get that you don't want to talk to me anymore, but I wish we could talk this out so we could be good and, like, move on."

DEREK. That's good, man.

MARCUS. That's not good.

EVAN. What?

MARCUS. It's not what he needs to say. Man, you gotta do better than that.

EVAN. I know!

MARCUS. So let me help you out, son.

EVAN. Really?

MARCUS. Yeah. Okay . . . (EVAN *gets ready to text her.*) Say this, be like, "Sonia, I want to apologize to you for the other night. I feel really bad about how things went down. You said you didn't want me to deep throat you and I did it anyway, and I know my apology isn't enough, but I'm truly sorry for sexually assaulting you."

EVAN. What the fuck?

MARCUS. Press send.

EVAN. Are you fucking crazy?

MARCUS. What?

DEREK. He's messing with you, yo.

EVAN. Why are you saying that?

DEREK. Ev, you know you guys are boys, he's fucking playing with you. Relax.

MARCUS. Your girl's down on her knees. You ask her to deep throat. She says no. You do it *anyway*. She fucking pukes and cries. What does that sound like to you? *(Silence.)* Derek, let's call your dad, the lawyer, and see what *he* thinks about this. *(Silence.)* Sonia's pissed, you shoved your dick down her throat and she didn't want you to. Man, imagine someone doing that shit to you? No big deal?

EVAN. But I really didn't mean to hurt her, I thought she was into it and—

MARCUS. Come on. *(Beat.)* Honestly, I'd fucking keep your mouth shut and hope she doesn't go telling all kinds of people, 'cause girls are not down with rapey dudes, you know?

DEREK. You're using the word "rapey" right now?

MARCUS. Why not?

EVAN. Should I call her?

MARCUS. No.

EVAN. Well, you're fucking with my head, man! I did not assault Sonia. You've never gotten so into it you kind of lost control? Man, it's not like I don't feel bad she's upset.

DEREK. I hear you, man. Fuck him, okay? I've definitely been there. Things get messy, what can you do, right?

EVAN. Fuck you, man. I'm not that guy.

MARCUS. You are a little bit though, actually.

EVAN. You're being a fucking dick.

MARCUS. I love you, bro. Just telling it like it is, is all. Don't call that girl. And you know what? I actually gotta peace. Evan, seriously, don't call her again or text her anymore. Act like it never happened and be done, bro. Or you're gonna be fucked. (MARCUS *leaves.*)

EVAN. Man, do you believe that asshole?

DEREK. I know. Man, I've been there. I just . . . I was hooking up with Kelsey this one time and it was like the third time we had sex or whatever and I was like, "You want to? You want to?" And she was like, "No, not really." And I was like, "Come on, come on." And she kept being like, "Nah," but finally she just turned over and let me do it. And she had a bad fucking attitude the rest of the day because she was like, "I didn't really want to and you wouldn't just leave me alone," you know? Just annoying. And she was all upset and I actually thought she was gonna be out, you know? But she got over it. But, like, you're gonna tell me that was some kind of violation? Nah. Come on.

EVAN. What is Sonia gonna do, man? Like, can she report this?

DEREK. No way, man. She wouldn't.

EVAN. Should we ask your dad?

DEREK. No.

EVAN. My mom would fucking kill me if this came out.

DEREK. Word, man. I feel that.

EVAN. I feel bad. I don't want Sonia to think I violated her.

DEREK. Yeah. *(Silence.)* I think she'll get over it. She's just feeling sensitive. Maybe she's embarrassed 'cause she puked.

EVAN. What about prom?

DEREK. Get a new date. Fuck her.

EVAN. I've got three weeks.

DEREK. Find a freshman band geek.

EVAN. I don't know, man. I guess I just fucked up, right? I, like, did not *want* to hurt her.

DEREK. No, man. 'Course not. You wanted to get off.

EVAN. I would fucking *never* do that shit again. 'Cause this is crazy.

DEREK. Honestly, just avoid her. It's probably what she wants.

EVAN. *(Looks at his phone.)* Fuck, I gotta go pick up my sister. Fuck. Is this bad? For real? Is she gonna tell someone?

DEREK. No man. You're good. You're a good dude, everyone knows that. You're not that kinda guy. This was like one weird fucking thing, let it go.

EVAN. All right. Thanks, man. Peace, yo.

DEREK. DC trip, man!

EVAN. Yeah. Tomorrow, bro.

(DEREK hangs for a second, gets out his phone, and makes a call.)

DEREK. Yo, Dad. Good. Yeah, it was fine. Dad, can I ask you something real quick? What makes something sexual assault? No. No, Dad. No, not even!

Don't worry, God, no. Jesus. I just gotta know for a school thing. (DEREK *exits in the midst of his conversation.*) Okay so, like, if a dude is, like, hooking up with a girl, right, and she's into it at first but then . . . (*As* DEREK *leaves the stage, house lights come up and* ANDREW *enters, addressing the audience.*)

CONFESSIONAL: ANDREW

ANDREW. There's a "dude" thing that I'm not sure I fit into, if I'm being completely honest. It's a fake-it-till-you-make-it situation for me most of the time. I try, you know? I try to, like, bro out with my friends but it's . . . I don't know. I just don't always want to do this shit. I don't want this stuff to be what we do whenever we're hanging out. It's fucking exhausting. And I say to my sister when she's like, "Why do you hang out with these guys?" I'm like, "Liz, what's my other option?" When you're a guy and you only have female friends, for example, you're gay, okay? I mean, not really, but in the eyes of, like, every guy you know, you're gay. If you're a guy and you're

in the drama club and you don't get
in on looking at nudes or a discussion
about whose vag fucking reeks—which
is just so offensive to me, by the way—
you're definitely a fag. And I don't even
mean a guy who likes guys . . . that's
not what I mean—I mean you're a
faggot. You're weak. You're not a man.
And I'm not saying I believe that—I
mean, I don't even use that word—
but that word gets fucking thrown
around constantly . . . at me, yeah . . .
and pretty much everyone . . . and
. . . and I do like these guys. They're
my friends. Would I be friends with
them if we were in college and I had a
larger pool of people to pick from? I'm
not sure. Probably not. And maybe I
sound like an asshole but . . . I don't
know. We went on this trip with our
U.S. history class last year. And I was
rooming with Evan and Nick—I chose
to room with them—but after curfew
they're like . . . *(Beat.)* Fuck, I feel like
I'm calling them out right now. I'm
not saying they're bad guys. *(Beat.)*
Whatever. So it was late at night in
our hotel room in Philly and they're
like, "Andrew, text Harrison and see
if you can get him to admit that he's
gay." "Andrew, text Luca and see if

you can get him to say he's a homo."
They were doing it too, to other guys,
but I think Harrison and Luca actually
might be gay. And I *know* Nick and
Evan think I'm gay—which I'm not—
so they were like, "They'll admit it to
you, Andy, they're way more likely to
admit it to you. Just tell them you're
gay too and it's okay. We know you're
not but just say it and it'll be hilarious.
Then we'll screenshot it!" And I did
it. Harrison and Luca didn't admit
anything. They didn't even respond
to my texts. They screenshotted it
and uploaded it to Instagram. Which
pretty much just cemented everyone's
theory that I'm gay. *(Beat.)* Sometimes
I just want to say to them, "The more
you talk about how much head you
get, the more you talk about the porn
you watch (and by the way, you're
staring at big dicks in all this porn
you watch, okay—how homoerotic
is *that*!), the more you talk about
what a man you are . . . *(*Derek *and*
Marcus *enter, carrying bags of take-out
Chinese food and* Andrew*'s computer
and headphones, which they set on the
stage left chair)* the more I start to feel
like *you're* overcompensating . . . for
something, bro.

SCENE 4. LIKE A VIRGIN

SCENE: ANDREW *enters the scene and sits with his computer on his lap and headphones in as the house lights fade to black. The only light comes from the video projection of a virtual tour of a hotel room. We hear elevator-type music or smooth jazz until a text conversation between* ANDREW *and his mom pops up:*

ANDREW. *We're here! Bus was fine. Room is nice but have to sleep on a cot. Chinese for dinner.*

MOM. *Glad you arrived safely. Try to make the most of it! Love you. Text me tomorrow. <3*

ANDREW. *Ok love you tell dad and liz i love them*

Lights up. DEREK, MARCUS, *and* ANDREW *sit in a hotel room in Washington, DC. They are all eating out of take-out Chinese food containers.*

DEREK. Yo, that's, like, your third egg
   roll, bro.

MARCUS. Why you keeping track of my
   food intake, son?

DEREK. 'Cause I thought we were
   sharing?

MARCUS. I said I'd share the lo mein with
   you—I never said shit about the egg
   rolls.

DEREK. Give me a fucking egg roll.

MARCUS. Don't ask me again. I'm serious.

DEREK. Gimme one. *(He goes to grab it.
   The two fight over the egg rolls for a
   second until they bump into* ANDREW.*)*
   Watch it!

MARCUS. You're being annoying.
   Grabbing at my shit—

DEREK. *(To* ANDREW.*)* Sorry, Andy.

ANDREW. That's okay.

MARCUS. Yeah, sorry A. *(To* DEREK.*)*
   Who paid for these? I did. So don't be
   touching my food. I even paid for your
   kung pao chicken because you spent
   your money on that piece of junk for
   Kelsey—your girl doesn't want a mug
   with the White House on it, okay?

ANDREW. You're wrong—she's definitely
   gonna want a mug. Kelsey loves coffee

and she's going to piss herself over the fact that you got it for her, Derek . . . *(He keeps browsing the computer.)*

DEREK. Thank you! Yes! Kelsey does love coffee. Don't be sad, yo. Don't be sad you don't have a girl to buy shit for.

MARCUS. Oh but I do. You. You're the little bitch I gotta buy shit for. What kinda man doesn't have his own money? And just saying—I got too many bitches—that's my problem. Cost me way too much to buy some key chains and shit for all of them.

DEREK. What about Sara?

MARCUS. I'm taking her to prom, aren't I? Hell . . . I'm her present!

DEREK. HAHAHA—that's hilarious. That's pretty much the funniest shit you've ever said. And I don't got enough to buy food on this trip because I spent my money buying weed last week and wait a minute, wait . . . did I or did I not share that shit with you?

MARCUS. Shut the fuck up.

ANDREW. Dude, can both of you shut the fuck up so I can watch this? And here, you want one of my egg rolls?

DEREK. See! Look at this! This right here—this is a friend, right here.

Sharing. Being nice. Thanks, man. *(He bites.)* So fucking good. Want some of my kung pao?

ANDREW. No, and seriously can you shut the fuck up.

DEREK. Okay, sorry! What are you watching?

ANDREW. *The Walking Dead.*

MARCUS. I want to fuck Maggie. Seriously.

ANDREW. Me too.

MARCUS. I'm in love with that girl. Fuck Glenn, you know what I'm saying?

ANDREW. Yeah.

DEREK. I kinda gotta thing for Carol.

MARCUS. WHAT?! Son!

ANDREW. You wanna fuck someone who looks like a grandmother?

DEREK. She's badass. Daryl's into her.

MARCUS. Maggie's where it's at on that show. Southern accent. And she's kind. She's exactly the kinda girl you should lose your virginity to, Andy. She'd show you just how to—

ANDREW. Why do you think I'm a virgin?

DEREK. 'Cause you are.

MARCUS. We're not busting on you, yo. Girls like that. Some girls like that, for real. They think it's cute. They want to teach you and shit.

ANDREW. And you guys have fucked countless girls, right?

MARCUS. Dude, come on.

DEREK. I can count them on, like, a lot of hands.

MARCUS. Of course.

ANDREW. Yeah well, kinda sounds like you're—

(Knock on the door. MARCUS goes to open it.)

MARCUS. Andrew, we're your boys, son. We're just playin'! You're a virgin and it's a beautiful thing. *(NICK and EVAN are at the door with small boxes of pizza.)*

NICK. Who's a virgin?!

MARCUS. You.

NICK. Yeah, right!

MARCUS. Nah, I'm playin'. Andrew.

NICK. Yeah. Hey, Evan's hymen's still intact too.

EVAN. Please, man. I'm not even gonna dignify that.

NICK and EVAN. *(To the other guys, everyone giving daps.)* What's up.

DEREK. What kinda pizza you got?

NICK. Mushroom.

EVAN. Cheese.

DEREK. Fuck that. I like meat.

EVAN. Yeah, we know. We've always known you like meat, dude.

DEREK. Hey Ev, does everyone know exactly how you lost your virginity? Don't be embarrassed, bro. Taking it up the ass still counts.

EVAN. If you really want to know the specifics on how I lost my virginity, man, ask your girl.

(Some snickering and then dead silence.)

DEREK. What?

EVAN. Text her right now . . . seriously.

DEREK. Wait.

NICK. Dude, come on.

MARCUS. Yo, I can't believe you're telling him like this? In front of all of us, man.

EVAN. Hey. You texting? She'll tell you all about it. Might make you feel like a little man though . . . if you know what I'm saying. Probably gonna make you feel micro, you know?

NICK. *(An aside to* EVAN.*)* How are *you* gonna make *him* feel micro?

EVAN. Shut the fuck up, man.

DEREK. Wait. You fucked Kelsey? *(Everyone breaks into laughter.)*

ANDREW. No. He's fucking with you.

EVAN. Man, you have got to chill about that girl.

NICK. This pizza is really fucking good.

EVAN. Seriously.

NICK. Okay, so you know what we should do?

DEREK. Watch *Walking Dead.*

NICK. No. After we're done with this, know what we should do? And, Andrew, you're coming.

ANDREW. What?

NICK. Rebecca, Victoria, and Frankie's room is down at the end of the hall.

ANDREW. So.

MARCUS. Yeah, so.

NICK. We should go hang out.

DEREK. What time's curfew?

NICK. 10:30. There's time. Let's just eat and go.

MARCUS. What's the point?

ANDREW. So he can see Rebecca.

NICK. No. I mean yes, but no.

EVAN. Getting Andrew some ass!

ANDREW. Nah, I'm good.

EVAN. Dude, you are not good. It's time. Junior year, man.

NICK. Rebecca told me Frankie's into you. No joke.

ANDREW. I know she is.

NICK. See! Dude, she's had a thing for you since you guys did the play in October.

ANDREW. I don't really give a shit.

MARCUS. Frankie's been looking good, actually.

DEREK. She's looking very good.

EVAN. I got a present for you, dude.

ANDREW. What?

(He flings a condom at ANDREW. *Everyone laughs hysterically—even* ANDREW.*)*

EVAN. Dude. Go. Get. Some. The girl is down. We'll go hang there and you can bring her back here.

MARCUS. Andrew, need me to teach you how to put it on?

ANDREW. Marcus, will you shut the fuck up, please?

MARCUS. *(As if reading a manual.)*
"When your penis is erect, you tear
open the packaging, and—"

ANDREW. I AM NOT FUCKING AROUND.

DEREK. Yo. *(Silence.)*

NICK. We're just messing with you, man.

EVAN. We just got your back, that's all,
and if you wanna stay a virgin, we get
that and whatever—

ANDREW. I'm not a virgin.

MARCUS. Come on?

ANDREW. I'm fucking not. I've said that to
you guys a couple of times—fuck. I am
not a virgin.

*(They all look around. Is he for real?
Then they celebrate.)*

ALL. Ohhhh!!!

*(They jump on ANDREW. Wrestling him.
Hugging him.)*

NICK. Man, this is crazy! Who is it?

EVAN. Georgia? It was Georgia.

MARCUS. Who?

EVAN. Georgia. Curly hair, sophomore,
smaller tits but banging body. She's
like cut—

MARCUS. Oh yes!

NICK. Georgia!

ANDREW. No—

DEREK. Dude, is it Kelsey? I know you guys are close and I'm down with that, but like, it's gonna be weird for me if—

ANDREW. No. Kelsey and I have not had sex.

DEREK. But you've done other stuff?

EVAN. Yo, shut up about Kelsey!

NICK. I seriously can't believe you didn't tell me.

ANDREW. Well—

NICK. I always, like, give you details. Dude, I show you pics. When did this happen?

ANDREW. I . . . I don't . . . it was a long time ago . . .

MARCUS. You gotta tell us!

EVAN. Yeah, man, this is the best news I've heard all fucking week, man.

DEREK. Yeah, come on.

ANDREW. It was a long time ago.

NICK. Over the summer? Was it that girl from the trip to Cali?

ANDREW. No. *(They're waiting in suspense.*

(ANDREW is hoping this shuts them up finally.) It was when I was twelve.

(There is silence. Until they all begin to go crazy with excitement—they literally begin humping things. Except MARCUS.*)*

EVAN. WHAT?! YO!

DEREK. He beat us all to it. We're fucking shitting on this kid and he's getting his nut off for the first time in, like, sixth grade!

NICK. Are you serious?

ANDREW. Yeah.

NICK. Who?

ANDREW. Diana.

NICK. YOUR FUCKING BABYSITTER?!

(Again, they erupt. They can't stop talking about it.)

EVAN. *(On his knees in front of* ANDREW. *Bowing down.)* Andrew, you are the fucking boss right now, man. You're, like, running shit, right now. I'm like—I don't even believe this! You fucked your babysitter?

DEREK. That's, like, every guy's wet dream right there? Is it not?

NICK. And you guys, she was the fucking hottest woman ever. She was like what then, Andy, nineteen?

ANDREW. Yeah.

DEREK. Dude, was it just the best thing of your life?

(Silence. Anticipating details.)

ANDREW. *(Not sure if or how to be proud of this. Trying to laugh it off.)* Aah . . . you know . . . yeah, I mean . . .

EVAN. What?

ANDREW. I mean yeah, it was good, you know? *(Trying to paint the picture. It sounds pornographic and that doesn't sit well with* ANDREW *but it does with the rest.)* I mean, she was, like, in charge and I still had a bedtime and, like, I was a fucking kid. And my sister's in the next room.

NICK. And . . .

ANDREW. And I woke up with her touching me.

EVAN. Oh my God, that's fucking amazing.

ANDREW. Yeah . . . *(trying to sound proud of this but failing slightly)* she was like on top of me and I didn't even talk and—

NICK. Oh my fucking God!

DEREK. Dude, why am I getting this sense that you really didn't like it?

(Silence. ANDREW is visibly confused—he's never said any of this out loud before. He feels on the spot and tries again to laugh it off.)

DEREK. Man . . . are you gay?

ANDREW. What?

DEREK. No, I'm just asking—

EVAN. Man . . .

DEREK. What?

NICK. Dude, you're—

DEREK. What? I'm asking if he's fucking queer because you gotta be gay if you don't absolutely fucking love being banged by your hot babysitter, I'm sorry. And he's acting like he didn't even—

ANDREW. No, man. I'm not gay.

DEREK. Okay, just asking! 'Cause it's weird, is all. I'd be shouting that shit from the rooftops.

(Silence. No one knows what to do. Awkward moment or two.)

NICK. So . . . should we go down the hall to the girls?

EVAN. Yeah, let's go.

DEREK. I'm down.

MARCUS. Yeah, let's break out. *(To* ANDREW.*)* You coming?

ANDREW. Nah. Just gonna watch.

DEREK. Okay, we'll be back before curfew.

NICK. Room 437 if you wanna come.

ANDREW. I'm good.

EVAN. Later, man.

(They all leave. ANDREW *is at a breaking point. He turns on the show and puts on his headphones.* MARCUS *comes back in and sits down.)*

ANDREW. What?

MARCUS. I'd just rather chill with you, if that's cool.

ANDREW. Yeah, it's fine. I'm watching.

MARCUS. That was some fucked-up shit.

ANDREW. What?

MARCUS. Your babysitter, man.

ANDREW. No. It was good—

MARCUS. No. And I wasn't gonna say it in front of them or nothing, but that's some fucked-up shit. And, like, I feel

you. I don't wanna get into it. But, like
. . . I seriously feel you. And you're my
boy, that's all. *(*ANDREW *stares at him
and then goes back to the computer.
Then* MARCUS, *breaking the tension . . .)*
But for real, are you gay? *(They crack
up.)*

ANDREW. Fuck you.

MARCUS. Fuck you too.

ANDREW. I'm pressing play.

MARCUS. Oh yes . . . now where's my
Maggie?

House lights come up as DEREK *enters
and speaks to the audience.*

CONFESSIONAL: DEREK

DEREK. Now, this is fucking awkward.
It's painful, actually. Oh God. *(He
laughs.)* Where do I start? I lost my
virginity to this girl Maggie when I
was fourteen. I was one of the first of
my group of friends to have sex, and I
was pretty fucking proud of that, you
know, but *(he laughs)* that's sort of
where my pride about it ends. This is
so embarrassing. Fuck. Um, okay . . .
*(*MARCUS *and* ANDREW *exit.)* So Maggie
and I had been talking for a while,

right? She was, like, a very cool girl—I was definitely into her. And we'd just, like, text all night—whatever—and we'd been hooking up a bit and stuff. And one day we're walking to school, oh my God, and she's like, *(he laughs)* she goes, "So when are you gonna take my virginity?" And I was like, "How 'bout today?" And she's like, "Where?" And I was like, "How 'bout my house?" And she was like, "Okay, do you have condoms?" And I was like, "I'll get some!" I seriously could not believe shit was about to go down, I mean, I was like busting out of my skin, you know? We left school early and went back to my place and I was trying to be all chill about everything, but, um, you know, I was fucking nervous. Oh my God *(he laughs)* . . . and I was all shaking while I was putting on the condom and I kept being like, "I'm not hurting you, am I? You're good, right?" Which was not like . . . "sexy" or whatever . . . I don't know. I finally get the condom on and she's totally down, and we're gonna do this. And we do it and it's kind of great—because I'm fucking having sex, okay? But, um, it was over in like . . . *(he remembers)* nine seconds. I sound like such a pussy right now, I know—man, I lasted nine fucking seconds. That's it. And she was like, "Uh, okay." *(Beat.)* And then it was mad awkward. She got dressed and said she'd text me later, and then she left. And she never texted me that night. So the next day I texted her and I was like, "Sorry about yesterday" and she was like, "It's fine babe" with, like, a heart emoji . . . but we pretty much stopped talking after that. She was just out. Done with me. I *did not* think it was gonna go down like that. No fucking way. No. I thought I was gonna be the man—just dominating the situation, and that did not happen . . . at all. But how would I have known any different, you know? It's not like my dad was like, "Son, your first time you pretty much come immediately—it's okay. You're normal. You're still a man." I mean, where is the porno where the guy lasts for nine seconds? Um, it doesn't exist. These guys are fucking for, like, thirty straight minutes without coming. What the fuck? They're taking Viagra or something because they're, like, not human! Even in *The 40-Year-Old Virgin*, they definitely make you believe Steve Carrell hung in there

for at least two minutes, you know?
No way you're doing it that long after
forty years of virginity. No fucking
way. So . . . whatever. Not good. *(Beat.
Remembering.)* It's not like that for
me anymore, thank fucking God! No. I
mean with Kelsey. I'm doing my thing,
you know. But, damn man, fucking
crazy humiliating. Maggie didn't tell
anyone, I don't think. I've been safe
from it getting out. And I got serious
respect for her for that. Man . . . so
embarrassing, actually . . .

SCENE 5. YOU'VE NEVER WATCHED FETISH PORN?

SCENE: *House lights fade. A video of the outside of* NICK's *apartment building is projected onto the screen. We hear sounds of a busy New York exterior. A text conversation between* DEREK *and his dad:*

DEREK. *Yo pops proof im at nicks. Sleeping here cool?*

DAD. *Good. Have fun. Text me in morning.*

Lights up on NICK, DEREK, *and* EVAN *at* NICK's *house.* EVAN *is sleeping on the central bench, which is serving as a bed.* NICK *and* DEREK *are on the seats, mid-conversation.*

NICK. So what else?

DEREK. Basically when I was, like, seven my mom was, like, this is too much, I'm out. And people don't think moms do that but, you know, they do. So. She just didn't want to do it. Which is fine. Like, you don't want to be in my life, then who cares, right? Fuck it. But my dad was, like, you can't just come pop back in and out of his life. If you're out, you're out. And she's been out. Done with me, you know?

NICK. Yeah, that's pretty much the plot of *Kramer vs. Kramer*. It's one of my favorite movies, man. You gotta watch it. It's streaming on Netflix now. Watch it for real. It's so good. And, like, the way the movie depicts the relationship between the dad, who's trying to figure it all out, and the son.

DEREK. Yeah?

NICK. Yeah, it's such good stuff.

DEREK. Nice. *(NICK's phone dings. He looks at it.)*

NICK. Rebecca.

DEREK. Tell her I say what's up. *(NICK types.)*

NICK. But that's basically the kind of movies I want to make. I really feel like all the action-heavy shit involves next to no storytelling. There's no depth—it's just the director and the special effects team masturbating and then jizzing all over us.

DEREK. Oh man, I totally disagree.

NICK. Really?

DEREK. Action is a genre, man. It's its own art form. Come on. *Inglourious Basterds, Kill Bill, Django Unchained*—all Tarantino's stuff— they have no story? Your argument is weak, man.

NICK. *Django* is totally a racist film!

DEREK. How you figure that?

NICK. White guys to the rescue, man! Are you kidding me? And it's sexist as hell, actually. And you know what, if Tarantino cared more about the story and fleshing out the characters, man, the movie would have more texture. And you could be like, "Oh yeah, this shit is violent—but at least it's not just gratuitous action."

DEREK. *Captain America, X-Men,* man—the, like, whole *Hunger Games* franchise. It's art. You don't have to like it, but it is.

NICK. Yeah. I guess. I just hate it. I would never want to make stuff like that.

DEREK. Top five favorite films—go.

NICK. Okay. Fuck. Let's see. Um . . . this is hard . . . *Annie Hall, E.T., The Shawshank Redemption, Birdman,* and *The Godfather Part II.*

DEREK. Okay, my turn—I hated *Birdman*, by the way, but whatever. So, I'm with you with *Godfather Part II*. So that's one of mine, then I'm also gonna say: *Fight Club*, *Training Day*, *The Dark Knight*, and *Kill Bill Volume 1*.

NICK. Okay. Yeah. I respect your choices.

DEREK. Oh, thanks, man. Thanks, Steven Spielberg. Appreciate it. *(Silence.)*

NICK. Hey, Evan, what are your top five? *(*NICK *and* DEREK *crack up.)*

DEREK. Man, it's only, like, 11:30. How the fuck is that dude asleep already?

NICK. I know, right?

DEREK. He's been stressing since the Sonia shit. Did he tell you about that?

NICK. No, not really—I mean, he didn't even bring it up in DC. I feel like people know something went down but no one knows the real specifics. Rebecca said Sonia's not talking.

DEREK. Yeah. That's a good thing, man.

NICK. And she's not going to prom with him anymore. Is that true?

DEREK. Yeah.

NICK. What happened?

DEREK. You know what, man . . . it's just a long fucking story. I feel bad for the dude.

NICK. What's he gonna do about prom?

DEREK. I don't know. He told me he might blow it off, but I don't know. I was like, invite some band nerdette or something. Who the fuck knows. But I want him to be there. Does Rebecca have a friend he could go with?

NICK. I can ask her.

DEREK. Yeah, do that. So, should we fuck with him right now?

NICK. Yeah.

DEREK. Should we put his hand in water?

NICK. What? So he'll piss himself?

DEREK. Yeah.

NICK. No! Is this a slumber party, man? Are you a seventh-grade girl?

DEREK. Okay—what about . . .

NICK. Oh, I know. I got it—I got it. Where are your headphones?

DEREK. *(He gets them.* NICK *gets his computer out.)* Right here.

NICK. Okay. Check this shit out. *(Pulls up the link.)* It's like . . . crazy shit, man. *(They watch.)*

DEREK. Oh my god. What is that? A choke leash?

NICK. *(Laughing hysterically.)* Yeah.

DEREK. *(Deciding to go along with the "hilarity.")* Fuck—this is some weird shit or something? BDSM shit. Whoa. *(They watch.)* He's, like, full-on choking her. And look at her, damn. *(Laughing.)* She's of course loving it. Freak.

NICK. How hilarious is this shit?

DEREK. So funny.

NICK. I know, right? And look at what she's got on. She's wearing fur. Like she's an animal. Man . . . watch this . . . watch this . . . *(They watch.)* This is so funny.

DEREK. Yeah.

NICK: So this is what we should do: let's put this right by him, right? Then we'll put the headphones on him.

DEREK: He'll wake up.

NICK: No he won't. He seriously won't. He's like dead when he sleeps, but we'll mute it until the headphones are on and then we'll unmute it and he'll wake up to this dude choking this chick dressed in fur who's screaming.

DEREK: Okay.

NICK: I bet this will make him piss himself. Seriously. Okay . . . You take this. I'll do the headphones.

(They set it up.)

NICK: *(Whispering now.)* Press play and then unmute it. (NICK *films the response.* EVAN *jolts awake and the first thing he sees is the video on the laptop and it freaks him the fuck out. He rips the headphones off and stares at the video and then at his friends and then back at the video.)*

EVAN: What the fuck is this?!

*(*NICK *and* DEREK *are laughing so hard they can't talk.* EVAN *stops the video.)*

EVAN: Seriously. What is this shit?

NICK: Man, that was amazing. I have you on video. Look at this. Look how freaked out you are. *(Showing them.)*

DEREK: That's great.

EVAN: That's not funny. Delete that.

NICK: Why?

EVAN: Because. I don't want that on your phone. Delete it.

NICK: No.

EVAN: Fuck you, man. Do it. Do it right the fuck now. *(NICK does it.)* What was that shit?

NICK. My brother sent me this link. And it's just some, like, fetish porn or whatever. Hilarious.

EVAN. So, what, you have fetishes now?

NICK. No, man.

EVAN. Maybe you do?

NICK. I don't.

EVAN. How many times have you watched that shit?

DEREK. I just saw it tonight when he showed it to me.

NICK. Couple of times. Sent it to some people.

EVAN. Fucking weird.

NICK. Oh please. You've never watched weird porn?

DEREK. *(Quick to flip-flop.)* Not that weird.

NICK. That's bullshit. You sent me that hooker porn link that time—with that girl getting gang banged.

DEREK. Yeah, well, that's not as kinky as this.

NICK. WHAT? Yo. Yes it is. It's worse.

EVAN. What would Rebecca think if she knew you watched shit like that?

NICK. I'm sure she knows I watch porn, dude.

EVAN. She knows you watch *that?* That's a whole different level of perversion, man.

DEREK. She would not be down.

NICK. Whatever, man. It's just a joke.

(Silence. They all go on their phones.)

NICK. I love how you act like you don't watch porn, like, three hours a day.

EVAN. I don't.

NICK. Okay.

DEREK. I watch an average of, like, thirty minutes a day, max.

NICK. An average. I know you marathon sometimes, man. We've talked about it.

DEREK. Sometimes. It's rare.

EVAN. Maybe that's why you have such a hard time kicking it to real girls, man.

DEREK. I don't.

EVAN. You do!

DEREK. What about Kelsey?

EVAN. That took you forever! Because she wasn't into it immediately, unlike every fucking bitch in your favorite pornos. She wasn't ready to get to it right away and you were like, "What?" And you were paralyzed. You were like, "Uh, uh, now what, man? The videos don't instruct me beyond this point. I'm lost and confused. I've got no game."

DEREK. Whatever, man. And you weren't getting your porn on when you deep throated Sonia?

NICK. What?

EVAN. Shut the fuck up, man.

NICK. That's what you did. Wow. Okay. That's fucked up, actually.

EVAN. Man, you've gotten head, like, twice in your whole fucking life, okay? Don't act like you know.

NICK. That's not even true, actually.

EVAN. Yeah, it is. And that shit with Sonia was a misunderstanding—I made a little fucking mistake. *(To DEREK.)* You really didn't need to bring that shit up.

NICK. What happened, exactly?

EVAN. I'm not talking about that shit with you, man.

DEREK. Hey . . . don't throw punches if
   you can't take 'em, son.

EVAN. Let's just stop talking now.

*(Big silence. All doing their own shit. It's
awkward.)*

NICK. Have you guys ever seen that,
   though?

DEREK. What?

NICK. *Deep Throat*. The actual *Deep
   Throat*.

DEREK. What do you mean?

NICK. It's a porno from, like, the
   seventies. Crazy retro. Linda Lovelace.
   You gotta see it. It's so stylized. It's
   when porn was actually artistic.
   Except, you know, the guy who made
   it, Louis Peraino, was an asshole—his
   dad was actually in the mafia. And
   then Linda Lovelace's husband was
   basically this abusive dick who was
   stringing her out and subjecting her to
   rape. And he would beat the shit out
   of her. Anyway, the film is wild and
   worth seeing. Original *Deep Throat*.
   Big-bush porn.

EVAN. *(Laughing.)* Big-bush porn. That's
   funny.

NICK. Yeah, she was also in a movie called *Dogarama*. She gets fucked by a dog.

DEREK. I've seen that before.

NICK. That movie?

DEREK. No. A woman getting fucked by a dog. When I was like seven, right? You know my cousin, Vincent?

EVAN. Yeah.

DEREK. I was like, in fucking second grade and he was fifteen, and he showed me this video of this girl working hard to get this dog to fuck her, and all these people are in the room watching and laughing and cheering for the dog and for her.

EVAN. For real?

DEREK. Yeah. And it was crazy because it was filmed in this, like, really nice apartment or house or whatever. Fancy.

NICK. That's crazy.

EVAN. Yeah.

NICK. You ever watched gay porn?

EVAN. What? No, man!

NICK. I mean by accident!

DEREK. No. I would fucking vomit if I saw that shit. Seriously.

NICK. Yeah. *(Beat.)* You think Andrew watches gay porn? *(They all burst into laughter for a bit.)*

DEREK. Yes.

EVAN. I bet he watches babysitter porn!

DEREK. That's fucking hilarious. *(Beat.)*

NICK. I showed him this link Marcus sent me of this girl getting fucked in an alleyway by a guy in a *Scream* mask—like, from the movie, right? Very dark shit. And he had, like, tears in his eyes. I was like, "Dude, are you crying?"

EVAN. Was he?

NICK. Kinda. *(They laugh.)* Rebecca watches porn.

DEREK. What?

NICK. Yeah. She told me.

EVAN. She's definitely not watching women fucking dogs.

NICK. Yeah, probably not. She told me when she first watched porn, it scared the fuck out of her. *(He laughs.)* The first time we hooked up she was like, "No matter what you do, do not cum on my face!" *(They all laugh.)* I was like, "No, I would never—but maybe on your stomach."

EVAN. You didn't say that.

NICK. I did. But as a joke.

EVAN. What she do?

NICK. She laughed.

EVAN. Like an actual laugh?

NICK. I think so.

EVAN. That's cool of her, actually.

NICK. Exactly.

DEREK. Kelsey wouldn't laugh.

NICK. Yeah, she wouldn't.

EVAN. Nah, she's a good girl. So is Sonia.

NICK. Yeah, man.

(Silence. EVAN lost in thought about Sonia. Then . . .)

EVAN. Okay, you know what? I think I'm just gonna head out.

NICK. Really?

EVAN. Yeah, man. I gotta get some good sleep and you guys messed with my head, man.

NICK. Dude—

EVAN. No, it's all good, man. *(Gets his stuff.)* Okay. I'm out.

DEREK. Peace, man.

NICK. Later, man.

(EVAN leaves. Beat.)

NICK. Dude, I gotta show you this *Deep Throat* video. You down?

DEREK. Yeah man, definitely.

NICK. You'll love the feel of it. Really fucking retro.

DEREK. Let's see some big bushes, man! (NICK *pulls up the link and gives the computer to* DEREK. *They watch for a little bit as the house lights come up.* NICK *walks downstage and talks to audience.)*

CONFESSIONAL: NICK

NICK. Basically, I would say I have good early game. Like, early into the whole relationship or whatever, not that it's, like, an official relationship, but you get what I'm saying, that's when I'm on point. Because I'm good at talking to girls—I'm a decent conversationalist, I listen, I'm genuinely interested in what they have to say, you know? No, seriously. And I'm not trying to be—you know . . . whatever . . . about this—I'm just being honest about what I think I bring to the table early on. If I go to a party, right, I can strike up a conversation about anything. I'm not intimidated by that aspect of it at all. Girls like to discuss movies and, like, feminism—done, easy—I can do that well. I'm a feminist. I want to be a filmmaker. I've got skills there. I can send witty texts. Like, short and smart. And girls are into it. I *know* they're into it because I *do* get girls—and maybe that surprises you— and fuck you if it does, actually. *(He laughs.* DEREK *exits with computer.)* But I get awkward in the transition. I could be better at advancing things from those conversations—those flirtations, right?—and the texting to, you know, the physical shit. I'm not bad at it. But I'm not great. And I'm just constantly struggling between not being a pussy and not being a weird, aggressive guy. Like, I'm not just gonna go over to a girl, talk to her for five seconds, and then put my hands all over her or pull her into a back room—that's fucking weird shit. And guys do that. Guys definitely do that successfully. Marcus—he's the type of guy who can do that without even hesitating. He just owns the situation. But if I were to do that, I *know* it would come off as creepy. And I want to be respectful too, you know?

But I also want to . . . you know . . . I want to, like, hook up with these girls. You know? That's not all I want—I'm not that guy—but I do want that and I fall a little short on making that move. And it's, like, what the fuck. Like, Rebecca . . . Rebecca was hooking up with this kid, Aiden, for a while. Even while she and I were, like, talking and whatever. And we'd all be at a party and she and I would be hanging out and then this douchebag would just come over and pull her away from me like it was child's play and they'd end up hooking up. And I remember being like, why the fuck can't you, like, be more aggressive? But aggressive is a very scary word. It might not even be the right word—confident, maybe? But I am confident. Ahh, I don't know. Empowered? No. That's like . . . that's funny. No. That's not it. But you get me, right? Maybe aggressive is the word. I've seen guys be heavily rewarded for being aggressive with girls and just being like, I'm into you, we're doing this, you know? It's a power thing and girls are attracted to that, I think. I'm not totally sure why, but . . . I mean, I'm with Rebecca now. So it worked out, but it took too long.

I looked like a fool to a lot of people in the process—and it's a little irritating to me that it took so much effort and that I don't naturally just know how to get things going. Fuck, you know? *(Beat.* ANDREW *and* EVAN *enter. Late night. After-prom. They drink from red Solo cups.)* I just want to find that middle ground where I'm still being, like, a decent guy, but I'm also getting what I want and, like, making effective moves—I'd be good with that.

(NICK *exits.*)

SCENE 6: BEST. FUCKING. NIGHT.

SCENE: *House lights fade and a projected video speeds us to the after-prom location.* ANDREW *and* EVAN *enter, wearing their suit jackets and holding red Solo cups. They meet center stage, share a handshake, and sit with their drinks. A text conversation between* MARCUS *and his mom is projected:*

MARCUS: *Sara loved the corsage! She's still wearing it at after-prom*

MOM: *Seeeeeeee! Your mother knows! Can't believe its your prom night! Love you! God bless you baby boy! <3 <3 <3 <3 <3 <3*

Lights up.

ANDREW. Amir and Erica looked good.

EVAN. Yeah, all coordinated—Erica slays, man—when she gets dressed up, right? Victoria and Bruno were too— but it looked cheap.

ANDREW. Yeah. Like very eighties but not in a good way.

EVAN. Your sister looked good. She looked like she was having fun.

ANDREW. Yeah, she was.

EVAN. Where is she?

ANDREW. She went home after. She didn't feel like hanging out with everyone, I think. Lots of people were going to Ted's and she was not gonna do that obviously.

EVAN. She didn't want to hang out with us?

ANDREW. I asked her but she didn't want to, so . . . you know. Where's Yolanda?

EVAN. Over there. Hanging out with Marissa Cortado. (ANDREW *looks.*)

ANDREW. I like her.

EVAN. Yeah, she's whatever. She's like a little kid. Freshmen. They're funny. They were in eighth grade less than a year ago! *(They laugh.)*

ANDREW. Did you talk to Sonia at all?

EVAN. Fuck no, man. Definitely not. Fuck her.

ANDREW. Yeah.

EVAN. She hasn't been talking to anyone about anything that you've heard of, right?

ANDREW. I don't think so . . . but I don't
really know.

(Silence. They drink.)

EVAN. Where you been lately? Feel like I
haven't seen you.

ANDREW. I see you every day in school.

EVAN. No, I mean, hanging out.

ANDREW. I've been busy with stuff. Play
rehearsals and whatever.

EVAN. Yeah. *(Beat.)* Can I say something
to you, man?

ANDREW. Yeah.

EVAN. You could have invited a guy, you
know?

ANDREW. What?

EVAN. Like, we don't care . . . you know?
You could have brought a guy to prom
and we still—

ANDREW. I'm not gay!

EVAN. Man, you brought your sister to
prom and, you like, never get with
anybody—

ANDREW. I'm so sick of this shit—

EVAN. And the whole thing with your
babysitter, I know you've had sex with
a girl—

ANDREW. I don't want to talk about that.

EVAN. But that was—

ANDREW. Why do you guys do this to me constantly? Why do you always fuck with me about this?

EVAN. I'm not. I'm just, like, telling you we're all good with it.

ANDREW. But I'm not gay. If I were gay, don't you think I would tell you?

EVAN. I don't know . . . I wouldn't.

ANDREW. What?

EVAN. I wouldn't tell us.

ANDREW. Okay, well—

EVAN. We can be dicks, is all I'm saying.

ANDREW. Yeah, I know.

EVAN. But I'm just saying—we're not homophobes or whatever.

ANDREW. I'm not gay. I don't feel like I should have to convince you guys of that anymore. How about that? I'm so fucking over being like, "I'm not gay, I'm not gay, I'm not gay." Do you know how often I have to fucking repeat myself?

EVAN. Why didn't you bring a girl to prom?

ANDREW. I did bring a girl.

EVAN. Man, you know what I'm talking about.

ANDREW. Because I'm not into anyone right now. And I didn't want to, like, be tied to someone all night. It's prom. It's junior fucking year. I wanted to hang out with my friends, not some random girl—like you have to do. And my sister needed someone to go with after everything and—

EVAN. Okay, A. Sorry. Forget it. *(They drink. Silence.)* So are you bi, then?

(DEREK enters.)

DEREK. What's good!

EVAN. Yo, what's up.

ANDREW. Hey.

DEREK. GOOD NIGHT, RIGHT?

EVAN. Yeah.

ANDREW. Yeah, it was good.

DEREK. *(Big announcement.)* Okay. Big news . . . I'm totally in love with Kelsey right now!

ANDREW. Right now?

DEREK. Yeah. *(ANDREW and EVAN laugh.)*

EVAN. Is she in love with you right now?

DEREK. Yeah.

EVAN. How do you know?

DEREK. She told me! She told me she loves me, bro.

EVAN. Wow.

ANDREW. I'm really happy for you guys.

DEREK. I fucking love her, man! *(EVAN laughs.)* What?

EVAN. Hey, if you wanna be cuffed, man, that's your business.

DEREK. Don't hate, man.

EVAN. Oh, I'm not hating—plenty of girls out there. Why you wanna be with just one, can't quite figure it out, but hey, you do you. Gonna be all pussy-whipped.

ANDREW. *(To* DEREK*)* Don't even dignify.

DEREK. Where's Lizzy?

ANDREW. Home.

DEREK. But at least she came, right?

ANDREW. Yeah. Did you see Ted body check me when we first got there?

DEREK. Yeah. I was watching. I would've had your back if things had gone down—you handled it, though.

ANDREW. He's a dick.

EVAN. *(To* ANDREW*)* Man . . .

ANDREW. What?

EVAN. I know I said it already, but I feel bad about the Lizzy thing.

ANDREW. You should.

EVAN. I know. And I do. *(They all drink.)* She tell you I apologized to her?

ANDREW. No.

EVAN. I did. I sent her a text. Shouldn't have done that to you, man.

ANDREW. Her.

EVAN. What?

DEREK. Man, you are just a groveling little bitch these days!

EVAN. Fuck you, son.

DEREK. But you are! You're like the Donald Trump of our school. Just offending *everybody*. No, wait, no—it's gotta be someone who's, like, done stuff to girls, not just said stuff. Like . . . who?

ANDREW. Also Trump doesn't apologize.

EVAN. Don't make me fucking beat your ass.

DEREK. Right. That's funny!

ANDREW. Anthony Weiner?

DEREK. What?

ANDREW. Maybe Evan's Anthony Weiner—the guy who sent the dick pic, remember?

DEREK. Um . . . no.

ANDREW. Bill Cosby?

DEREK and EVAN. NO!

DEREK: *(To ANDREW.)* You can't say that, bro.

EVAN. Fuck you—I'm done with this conversation. I'm gonna go find Yolanda. *(Goes to leave, but MARCUS dances in. EVAN brightens at the possibility of money coming his way.)* Yo! So what's the deal? Don't make my night worse, man. I'd love to go home with one hundred dollars.

DEREK. Yeah, 'cause he's not going home with anything else. *(EVAN playfully hits DEREK.)*

EVAN. I could get with Yolanda if I wanted—

ANDREW. *(To MARCUS.)* So?

(MARCUS takes a joint out of his pocket and lights it. Passes it. Milking it for all it's worth.)

EVAN. Yo, let's be men now, son—who owes who? Did you get her?

MARCUS. These girls, man. *(He laughs.)*

ANDREW. What happened?

MARCUS. Sara, man. Crazy.

EVAN. Fuck.

MARCUS. So . . . we're getting down, you know. And I mean, we're butt naked.

DEREK. How's the body?

MARCUS. Crazy. And I've got the condom on—

EVAN. She make you do that?

MARCUS. Yeah—it's not my thing but—

ANDREW. It's not your thing? This is why, like, 60 percent of people on earth have herpes, by the way.

MARCUS. Okay, so I'm, like, in. Okay? I'm talking, the tip is in. I'm serious. And I'm going real slow and working my magic and whatever because I can tell she's kind of nervous.

DEREK. *(Laughs.)* A "nervous slut." Oxymoron, anyone?

ANDREW. Dude, she's not a slut.

MARCUS. Yeah, man, I don't think she is, because she was like . . . fresh, if you know what I'm saying?

DEREK. What, like, her pussy was fresh smelling?

ANDREW. Oh my God.

MARCUS. No, man. Like, I think it was some uncharted territory, is what I'm saying.

ANDREW. You guys are fucking so—

EVAN. Do you owe me money, man? That's pretty much all I want to know right now.

MARCUS. And then she was like, "Stop."

ANDREW. What?!

MARCUS. Yeah, she was like, "Stop. Please stop. I'm really sorry. I don't think I want to. Is that okay?"

DEREK. No!

MARCUS. Right? And I felt like saying, "Fuck no, it's not okay! I'm partially in, girl, are you fucking kidding me?"

EVAN. So what did you do? (MARCUS *takes a hit.*)

MARCUS. I mean, what the fuck? It's, like, you're so into it, you're wet as fuck, the tip of my dick is *in* you and you're like, "Stop"? I was thinking, "Sorry, no. This girl has got to ease up and chill the fuck out and let's just finish what we started, right? I fucking brought you to prom, bitch!" Fucking annoying.

ANDREW. So?

MARCUS. "So?" Jesus, man, what do you think I did? Please!

DEREK. Pay the man. Both of you, pay him. Right now.

MARCUS. Nah.

DEREK. What? (MARCUS *takes another hit.*)

MARCUS. I just left.

EVAN. What do you mean?

MARCUS. I got dressed and walked out. She's over there hanging with Kelsey. Fuck it.

ANDREW. So you didn't fuck her?

MARCUS. Nah.

EVAN. (EVAN *and* ANDREW *celebrate.*) Hell yes! Gimme my hundred.

DEREK. You just gave up, bro?

EVAN. Pay up!

DEREK. All the situation needed was some finessing. You needed to finesse that shit.

MARCUS. Nah.

ANDREW. What did you say to her?

MARCUS. I said, "All good."

ANDREW. That's it?

MARCUS. Yeah. She was like, "Are you mad? Are you mad?"

ANDREW. What'd you say?

MARCUS. I was like, "Nah. All good."

DEREK. There's gotta be a girl you can get with tonight? Yo, call that girl Danielle, the one that works with you!

MARCUS. Nah. It's good. I'm a man, bro. I'm not a fucking destroyed little boy.

DEREK. Wow. You're such a sensitive guy, huh? You're getting all soft on us. You're giving up on getting some pussy, man, just 'cause your date got nervous! Sure you're not a homo?

MARCUS. Yeah, I'm a homo—I walked out on Sara tonight 'cause I really just wanna get with *you*, baby. Fuck you. *(EVAN begins to play "Bitch Better Have My Money" on his phone and holds it up to MARCUS's ear.)* Oh, I'm not paying you.

ANDREW. What the fuck?

MARCUS. Don't have it.

EVAN. Man! I *knew* you didn't have it!

ANDREW. Why the fuck did you make the bet, then?

MARCUS. I thought I'd win.

EVAN. I hate you, man.

(NICK enters. Drunk, but not too drunk. But definitely drunk. He dances full out while holding his red Solo.)

DEREK. Look at this kid!

NICK. This is a fucking great night. *(Takes a hit of weed from MARCUS.)*

ANDREW. Oh yeah?

EVAN. No it's not. It's fucking weak.

NICK. No, man. It's great. *(Chugs ANDREW's drink.)* I finally had sex with Rebecca.

ANDREW. What?!

NICK. Yeah.

(Big celebrating by all.)

ANDREW. When?!

NICK. Just now. It, like, needed to happen and it happened. And it was just—I fucking—I don't even know! *(Another hit.)*

MARCUS. That's fucking dope, son. Doing it!

DEREK. I'm proud, bro.

NICK. Thank you.

ANDREW. So where is she?

NICK. Still in the room. She's passed out. *(Laughs and drinks.)*

EVAN. What?

NICK. *(Totally caught up in the moment and loving it.)* Yeah, she was fucking wasted. We were doing shots when we got here and she's like one hundred pounds—dude, she's a serious lightweight. She was fucking shit-faced. *(Laughs.)* You should have seen her. You've seen Rebecca fucked up. *(Silence from the others.)*

ANDREW. Yeah.

NICK. Yeah. It was still good though, you know? *(Laughs.)* She's fine. She'll sleep it off. *(Laughs.)* Seriously, though . . . *(Silence. They all drink. Not knowing what else to do. Then . . .)* Best fucking night. Crazy. *(Silence.* NICK *basking in his success. He's busting!)* Like, I'm the fucking man right now, right?

(Big beat.)

ANDREW. I'm gonna go get another drink.

NICK. Yo, check on Rebecca for me?

ANDREW. Yeah. *(*ANDREW *exits.)*

NICK. Dude, isn't it weird he brought his sister to prom? *(Beat.)* Man, he's such a fucking faggot sometimes. *(Laughs.)*

(Fade to black.)

THE END

Production Notes

The staging of *Now That We're Men* should be organic, very physical, and fast-paced—keeping the focus on the actors, the text, and the power of the story. It became effective to create blocking based on the actors' improvised behavior and interactions when rehearsing. Actors should feel the freedom to play.

Set elements are minimalist: a bench and two chairs (rehearsal blocks, etc., can substitute). There should be no attempt to design sets for each location. Producers and designers should rely on sound, light, and projections to define and redefine the spaces.

Projections of texts are a challenging undertaking, but essential to the play. Smartphones and social media play crucial roles in the lives of young people like the characters in this play and offer insight into their lives that the text of the play sometimes can't. With each potential projection, *Now That We're Men* production and projection designer Daniel Melnick and I asked ourselves: *Why does this screen exist? What is the screen? Who does it belong to? What is revealed via the screen that propels the story forward?* To this point, we also chose to explore how the use of texting, social media, and video differ in peer exchanges versus family communication. We did not project any pictures during SCENE 2. YOUR SISTER'S TITS or video during SCENE 4. YOU'VE NEVER WATCHED FETISH PORN?—choosing to leave the imagery to the audience's imagination.

Throughout the play, each character participates in a "confessional" where he speaks directly to the audience, breaking the fourth wall. House lights should come up and the actors should be encouraged to enter the audience and engage with them fully. These are the only moments in the play where the characters are not performing for their friends, so the goal is to remove the element of performance. The CONFESSIONAL monologues are the most pure, honest, and stripped-down moments in the play, during which the characters reveal parts of themselves or struggles they're dealing with that they don't feel free to share openly with their friends.

There are a few cultural references in the play: Rihanna's "Bitch Better Have My Money," *Birdman* and other movies, the Jennifer Lawrence phone hacking scandal, etc. Throughout the development of *Now That We're Men*, we've had to update these references in order for the story to stay in the *present*—you should do the same. *Now That We're Men* tells the story of five male high school students; three were written specifically as African American. The race and class dynamics of this fictional group of friends was essential to the development of the script and its story.

The stories depicted in *Now That We're Men* are intense. They can be upsetting. The characters are in the midst of adolescence—sex, drugs, and drinking often dominate their conversations. The humor, vulgarity, and insecurity in the dialogue is the point of the piece and integral to its impact and value. *No alteration of the script may be made without written permission from Katie Cappiello.* Contact Katie with questions at NowThatWereMen@gmail.com.

Finally, engaging your team in conversations about *why* you want to produce this show should be at the heart of your process. I encourage all involved to research the subject as deeply as you can. A few suggestions to start are:

- *SLUT: A Play and Guidebook for Combating Sexism and Sexual Violence* by Katie Cappiello and Meg McInerney
- *The Mask You Live In*, a documentary from Jennifer Siebel Newsom
- Tony Porter's *A Call to Men* TED Talk
- *It Was Rape*, a documentary by Jennifer Baumgardner

Most importantly, talk to students, classmates, parents, and friends about the issues addressed in the play and listen to their stories. Gender norms, sexual shaming, and violence touch everyone, in complex ways. If you can give people a space to share and process, you are helping to make the world a better place.

Property List

Backpacks for all 5 characters

Bouquet of flowers (DEREK)

Phones for all 5 characters

Computer (NICK and ANDREW—used by other characters throughout)

Headphones (NICK and ANDREW)

Chinese take-out (DEREK, EVAN, and ANDREW)

Pizza (NICK and MARCUS)

Condom (DEREK)

Suit jackets for all 5 characters

Red Solo cups for all 5 characters

Joint (MARCUS)

Discussion Prompts for Talkbacks and Teaching Tools

Charlotte Arnoux and Katie Cappiello

1. What kinds of language and specific words are used in the play to degrade someone? Where do you hear these words? Where did you learn these words? Think of a time when you have used or been on the receiving end of this language. How did it impact you?

2. What norms (standards of social behavior) motivate the actions of our five main characters?

3. To which character did you feel the most connected? Remember, there are many characters that you don't see but who affect the plot, including Sarah, Liz, Sonia, Rebecca, and all of the parents. Which character's actions disturbed you the most? *Why* did that character do what they did?

4. Even though you may take issue with certain behaviors, do you like Nick, Evan, Marcus, Andrew, and Derek? Why or why not?

5. Do you feel differently about the characters in the beginning of the play than you do at the end? Which character's actions surprised you (in both positive and negative ways)? What sparked a shift in your feelings about them?

6. What cultural references to movies, people, songs, and events did you notice in the play? What

current events connect to the themes of *Now That We're Men*?

7. The characters in this play propagate a number of myths associated with sex, sexuality, and gender. What are some of these myths? Can you think of more? How are they learned and spread? How can we interrupt or correct them?

8. The characters strive to gain status from acting "manly": aggressive and wanting sex all the time. Why? How? Give examples from the play. How does this "act" play out in your world?

9. What is a sexual double standard? What are some stereotypes around sexuality and gender? How do race and economic status impact these stereotypes? What are some examples in the play and in the world? The truth is: sexual double standards and stereotypes negatively impact everyone. How and why?

10. Evan is humiliated in the locker room and told to "man up" by his father. His fear of not being "man enough" influences his actions throughout the play. How do deep-rooted standards of masculinity impact a young person's sense of self? Their sense of power? Their body confidence?

11. In the play, what words do the boys use to describe girls? Be specific ("your girl," "THOT-ty," "good girl," etc.) and think about what their language choices convey. Explore why the boys might chose to use this language when referring to girls—even girls they like or consider friends.

12. Among other epithets, the group of guys in *Now*

That We're Men playfully call each other "faggot." Is this word commonplace in your school or community? What does it mean? Does it affect different people differently (take the example of Andrew)? Is that important? Is it ever a victimless crime to use that word?

13. What role does virginity play in *Now That We're Men*? Describe the kinds of pressures placed on people of different genders regarding virginity in your own world.

14. Andrew and Nick have an argument on the subway when Nick reveals he has seen Andrew's sister Lizzy's nude photos, because a boy she liked (Ted) forwarded them. Do you empathize with Andrew, Nick, or Lizzy? Is it legal for underage people to send, receive, or pass on nudes? What should you consider when contemplating sending a nude picture of yourself or another person?

15. Nick defends Ted's actions by explaining that Andrew's sister, Lizzy, took the picture and sent it to Ted, and therefore the picture "became his." Do you agree? What should the *social* (not legal) rules around sending nudes be?

16. When Evan describes his "deep throat" moment with Sonia to Derek and Marcus, the two boys have very different reactions. Describe them. How does Evan attempt to justify his actions with Sonia? Does his defense sound familiar to you? Is it understandable? If yes, does that make them valid? Where do you think Evan learned about "deep-throating"?

17. Why does Andrew feel compelled to share the story of losing his virginity? What do the facts of this story tell us about Andrew's experience with his babysitter?

18. Describe the boys' reaction when Andrew reveals his sexual experience with his babysitter. Why do you think they react this way? Why does Marcus circle back to Andrew? Do you think the group reaction would have been different if Andrew had been female? How?

19. What happens between Nick and Rebecca at the prom after-party? How do his friends respond? If you were one of Nick's friends, what would your reaction be in that moment? What would you do with the information? How could Rebecca's assault have been prevented?

20. Why do you think some victims of sexual assault choose to never report their assault? What are the challenges that people of different genders, races, religions, and socioeconomic backgrounds face when coming forward?

21. Two girls experience assault in the play—Sonia and Rebecca. Take into consideration the race and class of all parties—Nick, Evan, Rebecca, and Sonia. What do you think would happen if Sonia reported Derek? What would happen if Rebecca reported what Nick did? Of the different scenarios, which one is most likely? What are the similarities and differences of these two sexual assaults?

22. What is pack mentality? Does it influence the

characters in this play? Give examples. How do you see pack behavior's impacting your world? Think broadly: politics, media, school, family life, sports, parties, etc.

23. What role does pornography have in this play? What effect does porn have on sexuality? How does it inform or influence standards for masculinity? What is the average age at which a boy sees porn for the first time? A girl? Are there any "side effects" associated with watching porn? What does Derek mean when he says to Evan, "And you *weren't* getting your porn on when you deep throated Sonia?" Does pornography fuel rape culture?

24. What does healthy sexual interaction look like? How is it achievable? How does it differ from sexual assault?

25. What are some examples in the play where each of the characters did *not* get or give consent? What is consent? Who is responsible for giving and receiving consent?

26. Technology impacts the way these characters communicate with others and explore sexuality. How?

27. Why do you think the playwright uses the device of "testimonials"—direct confessions to the audience—to tell the story of these boys? What are the differences in the way the characters talk and behave in the group scenes versus their "testimony"?

28. What obstacle does each character face in his attempt to just be himself? What are the challenges *you* face in your attempt to be yourself? Is "just being yourself" even possible? If yes, what conditions make it possible? And with whom?

29. Explore Nick's testimonial: Do you identify with anything he says? Are there any clues from his testimonial that foreshadow what lies ahead for him in the final scene?

30. In his testimonial, Marcus reveals he is struggling to balance expectations. What are those dueling expectations? How do they impact his decision-making?

31. How do cultural standards of masculinity play out in the homosexual and bisexual communities? How do they impact trans people? Genderqueer people? Intersex people?

32. The playwright specifies that Marcus, Derek and Evan must be played by African American actors. Why do you think she included this requirement?

33. Every scene starts with a text exchange between one of the boys and a parent figure. How do the parents and other adults instill unhealthy gender norms? What could they do better?

34. The lives of the characters go on after the play is over. What do you think happens to each character (including the unseen ones) after the prom after-party? What does the future hold for each of them—both long and short-term?

WRITING PROMPT #1: Write a note to your younger self. What advice would you give about gender, sex, and being yourself? Write a letter from your older self to yourself now. What you would call yourself out on? What would you be proud of?

WRITING PROMPT #2: What do you think is missing from the play? Write or improvise those scenes and/or monologues. Feel free to include new voices.

Good to Know: Tips for Leading Talkbacks and Discussions on *Now That We're Men*

Talking about masculinity, sexuality, families, and violence can feel very vulnerable. The following tips can set the stage for all parties to have an enriching and safe experience with this play and book.

Before a performance or group/class reading:

GIVE A HEADS UP ABOUT CONTENT AT THE TOP OF EACH PERFORMANCE. Keep it straightforward and short: "Thank you for coming. This play deals with rape and sexual violence." This is the moment to tell people to turn off their phones, too.

OFFER SUPPORT. If possible, have qualified counseling staff on-site to provide people a safe space to talk one-on-one if necessary. People don't often avail themselves of the resource, but they do appreciate knowing counselors are there.

GIVE PERMISSION TO LAUGH, CRY, GET ANGRY, BE OFFENDED. The play hits a lot of notes and sometimes people are afraid to respond naturally—so invite them to feel their feelings. At points, the actors engage directly with the audience, and it's fine to *participate* and respond (in ways that don't disrupt the production, of course).

Before a talkback or group discussion:

ADULTS, CHECK YOURSELVES. Don't lecture. Ask questions and be prepared to listen. Engage in discussions with an open, compassionate mind.

PASS THE MIC. Give everyone a chance to ask questions, voice opinions, and share experiences. Nothing should be off-limits as long as it can be conveyed in a way that is respectful.

They want to be found attractive and express themselves sexually without fear of being judged, and, like Nick, many of them want to have sex.

Searching for that "Middle Ground": Teaching *Now That We're Men* in a High School English Class

Carmen Julia Reyes

I had been teaching a course called "Gender and Literature" to seniors at Millennium High School (a public school located in lower Manhattan) for several years when a student of mine, Stella FitzGerald, invited me to see her perform in *SLUT: The Play* in 2017. Before the performance was over, I knew I wanted to bring this dramatic work into my classroom. During the talkback session following the performance, Katie discussed the need for young men to be part of the conversation about sexual violence and mentioned that she had written a companion play called *Now That We're Men (NTWM)*. Without having seen or read the play, I knew that it belonged in my curriculum as well.

Even though gender-based violence was an element in the literature I had been teaching in my twelfth grade English course, which includes works such as Shakespeare's *The Taming of the Shrew* and Jeffrey Eugenides's *Middlesex*, it was not a topic that my former students and I spent a lot of time discussing. Obviously, this would change by adding *SLUT* and *NTWM* to the course. In order to give myself, as well as my current students, the proper foundation for exploring such a sensitive topic, I assigned the plays at the very end of my year-long curriculum. This meant that we would read the plays in May, just when my students would be thinking about graduation, prom, and celebrating the end of their high school careers with parties that would most likely involve drinking and, possibly, sex. Just like the characters in *NTWM*, my students would be planning "promposals" and developing their own expectations for the night of prom. My hope was that by reading, discussing, and performing *NTWM* in English class, they would be more equipped to engage in honest conversations about sex and consent.

Before my students and I began our exploration of *SLUT* and *NTWM*, I thought it was a good idea to adapt some of the "Ground Rules for *SLUT: The Play*" from *SLUT: A Play and Guidebook for Combating Sexism and Sexual Violence*, which I consulted often and thoroughly recommend. Since I would be teaching the plays over the course of three weeks to three separate sections of "Gender and Literature," having counselors in the classroom was not practical. However, I alerted the guidance staff (well in advance) that my students and I would be reading and discussing potentially triggering material and that students who needed to talk to a counselor would be permitted to leave class immediately to seek support from the guidance office. I also spent time in class before the start of the unit, discussing the sensitive nature of the play and the need for the classroom to be a safe space where students could feel free to feel any emotion that the play evoked.

After setting these "ground rules" for the unit, I

continued to draw upon *SLUT: A Play and Guide-book for Combating Sexism and Sexual Violence* by having students read the extremely engaging essay "Who Really Benefits from Slut Shaming?" by Duane de Four. The connection between the essay and *SLUT* was immediately obvious to my students, but I also found that they referred to De Four's essay frequently while reading *NTWM* because of his discussion of words like "dog" that serve to perpetuate the idea that males cannot control their sexual impulses. Having read the essay, my students were able to discuss the language of the male characters in *NTWM* in relation to the various models upon which our cultural views of sex are based. Through a discussion of the music of Chris Brown and Lil Wayne, the essay also brings up the under-examined experiences of boys who were assaulted by an older girl or woman. Several students appreciated reading about this, since they felt the topic of sexual violence against men was one they rarely heard in the context of school or in the media. Not surprisingly, when they read about Andrew's experience with his babysitter in *NTWM*, they were able to identify it as rape and recognize the weight and empathy in Marcus's response, "I don't wanna get into it. But, like . . . I seriously feel you."

When it came to planning lessons for *NTWM*, I had to think about what I could accomplish within the timeframe of a fifty-minute class period, the fact that I had only one class set consisting of thirty-four copies (thus students had to read in class, rather than at home), and how to structure the lesson so that my students could walk away with at least one important understanding (or question) each day. I decided that we would read and analyze one scene per day. In some cases, we would consider the confessional monologues each character performs as its own scene to unpack on the following day.

Generally, the lesson would begin with students reading the aim or objective of that particular class (see Appendix A), which I wrote on the board each day, and writing a response to a prompt related to the scene they would be reading during class (see Appendix B). The next part of class was devoted to reading a scene. Working in groups of three to five, depending on the number of characters in the scene, students would assign themselves roles and read their parts out loud. For a few lessons, I decided to ask volunteers to come to the front of the room and read the lines out loud for the whole class. This variation allowed for all students to have a chance to read the parts of different characters and discuss the play with different members of the class. Allowing students to select their own parts for reading enabled them to choose a part they felt they could handle. And since students were not expected to perform or act their parts, I found that they were willing to try reading the parts of different characters over the course of the unit. Getting volunteers to read before the whole class was never an issue. When it came to the confessionals, which are the characters letting the audience in on their interior "real" feelings, I opted to read them aloud myself.

This seemed to help students focus intensely on the character's inner life and ensured that they would hear each confessional without any interruptions.

After the reading portion of the lesson, I asked students to engage in a discussion about what they just read or heard, sometimes providing them with specific protocols or prompts. Other times, I gave them a choice of questions or topics for discussion (see Appendix C). At various points in the unit, we stopped to hash out the definitions of specific terms like "rape" and "pornography" and to unpack the references to various films and songs that are mentioned in the play. Finally, class ended with either a full-class debrief or individual writing time, which seemed necessary for students to acknowledge and share their feelings and lingering questions. Overall, when it came to the lesson plan, my aim was to achieve a balance between structured writing and student-driven, open-ended discussions so that every type of learner would have an opportunity to experience the language of the play and talk about the issues that it raised for them.

Once we finished reading and discussing the play, there were only a few more days left in the school year. Prom was just one week away. I felt it was important for students to *make* something tangible that would continue the conversations *NTWM* had started. Thus, I offered students four options for their final assignment, which could be completed individually, in pairs, or in groups:

A. Is there a character or issue in *SLUT* or *Now That We're Men* you would like to explore further? Create a script or monologue for either one of the plays.
B. Create an action plan to help our school community address sexism and sexual violence.
C. Create a PSA poster to raise awareness of sexism and sexual violence.
D. Create a playlist of songs to accompany our study of the plays. Provide a brief rationale for your choices.

I was amazed to see how willing, even eager, these seniors in their last week of classes were to create and share their final assignment. Gratifyingly, all students were able to demonstrate their understanding of at least one of the play's messages about sexism, sexual violence, and more, while also producing creative work that could be passed on to future students and the larger school community. The connections that I hoped students would see between gender, literature, and their own communities at the beginning of the school year were made crystal-clear through their own artwork, dramatic works, musical compilations, and action plans.

There is no way to summarize all of the diverse ways in which my students responded to reading *NTWM*. I saw expressions of amusement, shock, recognition, sympathy, disgust, embarrassment, disbelief, and confusion. Reactions to individual characters were also extremely varied. What remained consistent across all of my classes was the response to the play's ending, where the character of Nick recounts that he and his girlfriend just "had sex" while she was passed out drunk. Students reacted to sexual assaults earlier in the play, but their reaction to Nick was more intense.

Why? Because this is the rape that ends the play. My students were familiar with the definition of rape and had no trouble identifying Nick's act as such. But another reason may be their identification with Nick's search for a "middle ground" between too-passive and too-aggressive with romantic interests, which he describes in his confessional before the final scene of the play. One student explained to me his shock, "he called himself a 'feminist,' so I was not expecting him to just take advantage of a girl. . . ." Another student wrote, "After reading Nick's confessional, I sympathized with him because it's a natural problem guys go through. But, after finishing the play, I've never been more disappointed in a character. Nick raped Rebecca on prom night."

Indeed, at first many of my students expressed sympathy for Nick. Like him, many of them regard themselves as feminists and critique sexist movies and stereotypical characters that reinforce gender norms. They joke around with peers and use words like "slut" and "player" with a sense of control over the meaning of those words from within the safety of their friend groups; at the same time, they acknowledge the problem of slut-shaming and see how those words help to sustain it. Like Nick, many of them find searching for that "middle ground" to be a challenge. They want to be found attractive and express themselves sexually without fear of being judged, and, like Nick, many of them want to have sex. They are scared of rejection, like Nick, and envious of what seems like girls' double-standard with smooth guys like Marcus. And, just like Nick, many of them drink, especially on an occasion like prom night. So, I can only imagine that the strong reaction I witnessed to Nick's drunken celebration of rape was partly a deep-seated fear that they, too, could lose themselves and hurt others in their search for that middle ground.

This fear is important to acknowledge, and yet can be so hard for teenagers to talk about. I am grateful that *NTWM* ends in this disturbing ambiguity. We don't hear Marcus or any of the other characters reprimanding Nick—their silence speaks volumes—and we are left to wonder how, or even if, Nick and Rebecca, as well as the other characters, truly understand what happened on prom night. One of my more pessimistic (or, you might say, realistic) students wrote, "I think the reason why the ending was not how everyone pictured it to be is because life goes on. It doesn't matter that the guys confessed [their vulnerabilities in the monologues]. At the end of the day . . . these behaviors will continue. . . ."

Being the idealistic English teacher that I am, I have to disagree. Yes, life does go on, but plays like this change the way we go about our own lives. In the context of my English class, the play gave me a way to have meaningful and practical discussions about consent, alcohol, and ways of staying safe with people who I want to help thrive. As I write this, prom night is over, and my seniors have graduated. I have no doubt that the conversations they started in English class will continue.

Appendix A: Lesson Aims

1. What matters to Marcus and his friends, and how do they express this?
2. How might our parents' ideas about gender affect us?
3. How should we treat nude pictures that are shared with us?
4. How do Marcus and Derek react to Evan's "interaction" with Sonia, and what do their reactions imply?
5. What "kinda guys" (that is, male stereotypes) are there?
6. What does pornography teach about sex?
7. Why is it so hard for Nick to find that "middle ground"?
8. What does the play leave us thinking and feeling? (And what can we *do* with these thoughts and feelings?)

Appendix B: Writing Prompts

1. What does the term "promposal" suggest or imply? What makes a "promposal" successful?
2. What would you like to say to Evan and/or his parents?
3. What feelings does Marcus's confessional bring up

for you? What do you think Marcus means by "circle of bullshit"?

4. Derek says to Evan, "You're not that guy." What does he mean and how do you think this makes Evan feel?

5. Think about some of the shows or movies you've watched recently. What do they "teach" about sex and gender?

6. What words stand out to you in Nick's confessional? Why?

Appendix C: Student-generated Discussion Questions

1. Can we consider any of the characters to be feminists or even "decent" guys? Do any of them genuinely respect women? What should they do in response to Nick's rape of Rebecca and Evan's rape of Sonia? What will happen to these "friends" as the school year ends? How can they become the men we hope they'll become?

2. How does the play treat male rape?

3. What's the role of alcohol in *SLUT* and *Now That We're Men*? Can you have consent when you and/or your partner is drunk?

4. Insecurity seems to play a major role in the play. Why are the guys so insecure? Are the young women in *SLUT* insecure for the same reasons? Do different genders cope with their insecurities in the same ways?

5. Did Nick really believe what he said in his confessional? If so, why did he rape Rebecca? What is the

purpose of the confessionals? Did they enable you to sympathize with or understand the characters more?

6. In what ways do *SLUT* and *Now That We're Men* reflect the attitudes, feelings, behaviors, etc., of students at *this* school? How would the play be different if it was set at our school?

James and I were kids. I wish we could've just been allowed to *be* kids, because our innocence was all we had.

Elementary

Alphonso Jones II

James Harris and I met when we were placed at the same table in our kindergarten class. We both had fun-loving, goofy personalities and eventually began to hang out on the weekends. I'd go over his house more often than he'd come to mine, but our parents knew each other and, at one point, I saw him as a brother to me.

What made James different from all the other boys was his habit of gesturing dramatically when he spoke. He'd roll his eyes, wind his neck, snap his fingers, clap his hands, and sometimes smack tables in heated conversations. This behavior mirrored the girls our age, and it confused me to see him act like that. *What's wrong with him? Why does he act like a girl?* I wondered, and, *How can I get him to act like a boy?* In actuality, there's no one way a boy or girl should act at eight or nine years old, but what I now know are societal gender norms convinced my young mind that my best friend was not emitting male behavior. Therefore, he must be—you guessed it—gay.

I blame my elementary school ignorance for the actions that followed. By the first grade, we were still in the same class, but I began to adjust the way I interacted with him in order to treat his overtly feminine personality. I would, for example, force on him the idea of females being sexual objects to conquer, manufacturing feelings between him and the girls in our class. Playing Cupid wasn't enough to change James, so I did something I look back on now with guilt.

We were at his house one day when I decided to use his computer to look up some porn. There wasn't any ill-intention or bullying going on in that moment, just me trying to show a friend the right way to be. I honestly thought I was helping him. He was so uncomfortable, I feel shame when I think of it now, but back then I was oblivious. I recall adamantly telling him, "Look, you *need* this. You need to look at this. This is what you want." He ran away from the computer and I eventually stopped looking.

The idea of using hardcore porn as a teaching device is baffling to me, because what the hell was he going to learn about being a man or anything else from aggressive sex on a computer screen? Porn wasn't anything new to me because I had seen it time and time again at my cousin's house. In fact, that's where I had learned the lesson I was trying to teach him about sex and how you treat girls. But the truth is, I was upset, inside, when I first saw porn and I forced my trauma onto him, creating more trauma all around—all in an effort to "be a man."

Our friendship fell out after a few years. James matured, eventually simply growing out of flamboyance and into quiet mellowness by high school. What I did to him definitely impacted his life, though, and it left a permanent mark in my memory. I don't believe he was even gay. He was just a boy who felt liberated to act in a way that was natural for him—and I was supposedly his friend, but I didn't have his back. He wasn't a macho eight-year-old, but what man can say that they were? I look back to my own young life and see how I was forced to act a certain way, how my behavior was policed by adults, teachers, and older children. James and I were kids. I wish we could've just been allowed to *be* kids, because our innocence was all we had.

Now I'm in college. It's not acceptable to me to be around people who want you to be who you aren't or who think it's funny to make rape jokes. I am hyper-aware of how I choose my friendship circle. I need to have some way to make sure the people around me share my values without seeming weird. This can be hard to do. You don't want to meet someone and have your first conversation be about porn or sexual assault. That said, natural tests that illuminate where a person's heart truly is often seem to come along in the nick of time. Sophomore year, I found myself in the midst of one of these tests.

My friend Josh oversees the university game room as his work-study job. I frequently hang out with him there to pass the time while he works. In the middle of one of our meaningless conversations, another guy, who Josh knows, sat down after finishing a conversation with a pretty girl on her way to the treadmill. Josh asked him, "Is that you, bro? You working on that? She like you?" The guy said, "*Ehh*, she's a bitch." I said, "Why, because she's not making it easy for you?" To which he responded, "No, she's just a bitch. But that girl right there"—he pointed at a blonde girl on a treadmill next to the first girl—"you get *her* drunk enough, you can fuck her." He smiled.

It got quiet. I actually don't mind being the "preachy" dude who stands up for what's right, but I wanted to see if I really had to be the one to burst this bubble—or if someone else would speak up before I had to say anything.

After a pause, Josh said, "Isn't that rape?"

I chimed in, "Yeah, bro, that's rape. You just said if you get her drunk enough *you* can fuck her. That's not right. Have you done that?" The guy tried to back out of what he said, but once he realized how bad he looked at that moment, he left.

It's good to know that there are other guys, like Josh, who understand consent and proper sexual conduct and don't mind checking other guys on it. I hope that that the other guy never hurt anyone, including himself, with the logic of getting a girl "drunk enough" to have sex. In my mind, he is a victim of toxic masculinity, too; if he wasn't, he would know that giving anyone alcohol to the point of drunkenness and then having sex with them is not okay—it's rape. I hope he took that lesson about rape to someone else who didn't know as well. "Each one, teach one" is the only way for this message to be spread among men. As tough as it may be, it's important to speak up when you hear guys minimize or endorse rape, no matter how they couch it, and no matter whether you're the lone voice.

I was willing to be that lone voice in the game room, but I'm glad I didn't have to be.

We're taught that to be a man is to control everything around you, even if that includes other men.

Gamer Shame

Isiah Rosa

I get home from work and feel like I need to relax. I turn on my PS4 and put on my headset. After looking at my dashboard for a few minutes, trying to determine what to play, I hear a chime, and an invitation for *Fortnite* pops up on my screen. It's my friend, Michael, in a party with my other buddies, Surendra and Divindra. It seems as if they're expecting me, so I boot up *Fortnite* and join their game.

In the lobby, my friends' chatter dwindles and transforms into greetings as they notice I have arrived. I greet everyone, ask them how they're doing. We've all had long days today, so now it's time to try and capture the elusive "Victory Royale!" We ready up and enter the game. Michael starts joking around with me. "Yo, Isiah, you tryna be my bitch tonight?"

"Nah," I retort. "After I carry the team this game, you're gonna be calling me Daddy." The whole crew laughs, and we continue with the game.

As we play, more of these implicitly homosexual roasts populate our banter. Sometimes they are a little more explicit, and these back-and-forths make up a considerable amount of our gameplay chatter. When we're not calling out enemies, or giving each other tips, we're cracking dick jokes and joking about fucking each other. Of course, we know not to take it seriously, and even though I know that making these jokes can be considered homophobic, I do it anyway.

But why do I do that?

I've thought about this a bit. Because I have been immersed in gamer culture since a very young age, I consider using these slurs to bond normal. Normal within the context of playing with friends who I trust, that is. If I were to act this way in public, it would be gravely inappropriate. That said, when I'm playing with my friends, and it's just us, the filters disappear. No one cares about checking someone for saying something out of line. No one gasps if what we say is wrong or inappropriate. All that matters to me and my squad in that moment is having fun and winning our games.

We don't make these jokes and roasts because we hate gay people, either. They occur within a contest of power among ourselves, constant back-and-forths in order to determine who is the alpha male. Whoever has the last word, or whoever makes the most clever or stinging roast, is deemed winner, and the winner changes every time we play.

This need to dominate one another through humor is socialized within us from a young age, as far as I can tell. We're taught that to be a man is to control everything around you, even if that includes other men. These roast sessions are a manifestation of the warped masculinity that resides within me and all my gamer friends. We all feel some need to be on top and playing competitive video games like *Fortnite* fuels that fire.

Even though I partake in these verbal wrestling matches and even defend them, I understand that there is a lot of nasty shit within the gaming world that needs to be cleaned up. For example, it's very difficult for women to break into the industry. I didn't know of any female game designers until I learned about them in one of my college courses. I should not have to take a college course to hear about women's experience or impact in the game industry; they deserve the spotlight just as much as their male counterparts. I consider myself a feminist and can see that there needs to be a shift in order to make the game industry more inclusive—in terms of gender, sexuality, and race.

How do we make that shift? It's not as easy as flipping the narrative and women dominating the industry. The solution to dismantling the patriarchy within gaming is not building a matriarchy. Instead, we need to support this shift naturally by encouraging women to enter the industry and not harassing them (#gamergate) when they do. Women can tell stories that men cannot, and those unique perspectives are potential ideas waiting to be harvested. The next *Legend of Zelda* could lie within the mind of a queer black woman, but we may never hear about if it remains so much harder for her to make it as a game designer than it is for a straight white man.

We can accelerate this change by giving these women better access to opportunities that can allow them to enter the industry. Opportunities like summer programs, college programs, and initiatives of that nature will work wonders for the diversity of the gaming world. In fact, they're already working. At NYU's Game Center, my class of 2021 is majority female. It's exciting to know that my generation will be the one to spur evolution and seed the feminist future of the game industry, but right now that evolution is nonexistent.

Currently, some of the best-selling video games on the market capitalize on intense violence and toxic masculinity in order to drive sales. *Grand Theft Auto* and *Call of Duty* make millions of dollars by catering to their primarily male audiences. The teams behind these successful games are typically male, so they create experiences and stories that reflect their own. But women make up 45 percent—nearly half—of all gamers. That is a huge population of people that are not represented in games. The disconnect is stark, and it leaves women gamers unsatisfied, offended, and disrespected.

The men leading these best-selling game studios may not want women to be a part of their team. They may believe that allowing women to help create their games may put a damper on their lucrative, disgusting ideas. They will no longer be able to freely objectify and marginalize women through their games if there is a woman helping make that game, and, frankly, they may not want to lose the privilege. (As Gamergate makes clear, many men worry that without sexist hostility keeping women out, they can't be successful.) The conventional wisdom is that when women join these game studios, the games will become soft and uninteresting. To me, relying on sexism to create a game is the least interesting thing one can do.

One reason we don't see many female game designers at the forefront of the industry is that it means women would be forced to work within an industry that capitalizes on their marginalization. Why would a woman want to help make a game that perpetuates unhealthy and oppressive ideals like toxic masculinity and rape culture? I'm interested to see women of all backgrounds and communities dive into the indie game scene, make something nobody has ever seen before instead of *Boring Shooting Game 2: The Shootening*. That act of rebellion will help diversify the industry and bring new faces into the fray.

The same logic can apply to my friends and I when we play *Fortnite* and slap each other around with homophobic slurs. We would be a lot more hesitant to say problematic things if a girl were to join our game and listen to our chatter. Suddenly, we would be checking ourselves before telling a joke or making a roast. *Is this okay to say? Will I offend anyone? Is there something more creative I could say to get my point across?* The moment a girl enters our masculine bubble, we hit the brakes on what is clearly bad behavior.

I get home from work and feel like I need to relax. I turn on my PS4 and put on my headset. After looking at my dashboard for a few minutes, trying to determine what to play, an invitation for *Fortnite* pops up on my screen. It's my friend, Michael, in a party with my other buddies, Surendra and Divindra. I boot up *Fortnite* and join their game. I realize that, though making the adjustment might be a bit awkward and uncomfortable, it'd be nice to take a break from being problematic. I try it. We are conscious of our words and the larger world when we play. No one is trying not to be anyone's bitch tonight, and it's a relief.

I always had to worry about appearing weak, feminine, and somehow wrong.

Dude, Are You Going to Cry?

Jordan Eliot

My mother is a therapist. Because of this, I was taught to cry as a kid. I never had to prevent a single salty drop from sliding down my flushed face. Weeping was not just acceptable, it was admirable—a simple and effective way to express emotion and begin to move past whatever was hurting. For the first few years of my life, I had no idea that crying was shameful.

The unfortunate truth became apparent in the first grade, during recess. Everyone was released to the playground, but I was "benched"—sentenced to sit on a bench in the yard and watch everyone having fun without me—for being too noisy in the cafeteria. As I sat, devastated, I could feel the hot liquid pooling on my lower lash line, about to take the familiar plunge down my cheek. My lunchtime exuberance was my first offense, and "benching" seemed to me a too-harsh punishment.

Just then, Dylan and Sean—my new friends— headed towards me, zipping effortlessly across the yard past the gap in the concrete where I routinely tripped. They took one look at me and threw their heads back, releasing cackles from the meanest part of their innards. "Dude, are you going to *cry*?" I froze, stricken. *Yes. So? Oh, wait . . . .* A new reality dawned on me. I took a deep breath and vacuumed the tears back into my head. I learned my lesson.

This lesson followed me like my own shadow. Except, the older I became, the more I realized crying wasn't the only crime in my repertoire. I didn't have to get moist-eyed or visibly display any sensitivity to be berated for just that—I'd be punished if I wasn't, openly and proudly, a macho dick.

In the groundless beginnings of my freshman year of high school, I scrambled to find a friend group and latched on to the first people I could find. We were an unlikely trio: Cam, Kevin, and me. I hoped their bold ease and self-assurance would rub off on me. Sure, Kevin had been my worst nemesis in the sixth grade, which didn't bode well for intimate friendship, but I was determined to make this work—people deserve second chances, after all.

The first time we all hung out, things started off great. It was the first Friday of the school year, and autumn's slight chill was beginning to infiltrate the air. We were hanging out in the park closest to school. Of course, the topic of girls came up. The conversation began in a relatively tame manner. We all shared the girls we were beginning to like—bonding over any overlaps.

Kevin, who had become the unofficial leader of the group, shushed us all, chuckled, and said, "Okay, but if you had to *rape* someone in our grade, who would it be?" There was silence. And then some more. Cam was supposed to share his choice first, but he looked confused and disturbed and didn't make eye contact with any of us. After a bit, Kevin rolled his eyes, scoffed, and said something I knew wasn't quick-witted, even back then: "Why don't you save those tears for the pussy convention? I was just joking."

The mood of our hang regained its light-heartedness after that "scintillating humor," but I could tell Cam was a little shaken. The truth was, I was, too. Kevin's question was so offensive, but the idea of calling him out seemed impossible. It wasn't something I would ever dare to do.

In that moment, the sin of crying had been replaced with the breach of not going along with whatever crazy shit other guys said or did. But the consequences were the same: humiliation. One slip-up, one moment of feeling sadness or shock or revulsion about a rape joke, and you were taken *down*. In this new social scene of high school, we either had to blindly follow our friends *or* come up with something funnier or wackier in response. It was a constant competition. We were always testing each other. Who could we make squirm? Who could we take down in order to build ourselves up?

Not even Kevin was immune. I knew his rape question was an attempt to get us all to bond by laughing, essentially, at girls—to have our giggles feed his appetite to feel on top of the world at all times. I knew his pussy remark after Cam wouldn't answer his question was just an attempt to save face—to make sure someone else felt destroyed before we had the chance to call him out on his shit, because that would be humiliating for him.

After a few weeks of trying to be bros with Kevin, I decided I could not stomach his compensatory behavior. The last straw is hard to pin-point: Perhaps it was the unsettling photo he showed me in biology of conjoined twins giving some guy a blowjob. As excruciating as it was to be friends with him, I was scared to cut him off. What would it mean for *me*? What would he say about me and my unwillingness to participate in his code of conduct? I consider myself really lucky that I had Cam in my life, because he was just as sick of Kevin as I was. We both stopped hanging out with Kevin at the same time, and Cam and I are friends to this day.

Kevin, on the other hand, found plenty of other people willing to compete with him to be the top dog. It looked fun to be them from the outside, but I remembered what it felt like to be friends with him. It was like walking on eggshells. It was like skating on thin ice. It was exhausting. I always had to worry about appearing weak, feminine, and somehow wrong.

Looking back on it all now, though, I wonder if Kevin was hurting the most. There was never any space for him to discuss what was going on in his brain—which we all know is a cesspool of insecurity in high school, regardless of who you are. None of us ever felt safe enough to reveal our struggles to *anyone*. I was lonely. It was certainly possible that Kevin was, too. We had to constantly prove ourselves to people whose approval we desired, but who we didn't respect, always moving further and further from revealing who we really were. We were all trying to make sure we never appeared weak or sensitive—and we fed into a vicious cycle that rewards behavior that is degrading and really has no benefit for anyone. My experience of high school socializing is really common, and that fact makes it feel even more unfair and sad.

So sad, in fact, I think I need a good cry right now.

When I am describing male bonding to these men, I say that it means that the biggest jerk in the room sets the norm—not the most thoughtful guy, the most interesting, the most engaged.

Bro-cialization

Peter Qualliotine

Recently, at my local Seattle food co-op, I stood next to a middle-aged white guy (like me) at the herb counter. He was (like me) scooping herbs from a jar into a small plastic bag—a couple of progressive dudes doing their shopping. Along the wall across from us were the bulk bins of flours, nuts, seeds, and other assorted natural foods. A co-op employee was refilling one of the bins, bending over with her back to us. Then, the guy turned to me, nodded in the direction of the young employee, and said, "I wouldn't kick that out of bed!" My heart sank. I wasn't surprised, but I was sad and annoyed. This experience—a guy trying to do the male bonding thing with me—happens a lot.

When I use the term "male bonding" here, I'm not talking about establishing deep, fulfilling friendships between men, relationships that are rooted in mutual trust, respect, authenticity, and love. I'm not talking about anything that represents true *philia* connection. No, I'm talking about connections forged by the rules of "masculinity," that uneasy truce between men that mimics real relationship. This socialization into performing male supremacy—bros before hoes— is rooted as much in a fear of other men as it is in misogyny (the hatred of women) and homophobia (the irrational fear of gay people, often accompanied by anxiety about being perceived as gay). Neutralizing hostility between men often requires a tacit agreement to participate in the subordination of women; this is how the charade of manhood is made real to one another, and to oneself.

Bonding at the expense of women is a patriarchal mode of being that primarily oppresses women, but it also drives the desperation, alienation, suicide, substance abuse, depression, anger, and plain loneliness of so many men. It turns some of us into shelled creatures lacking the social and emotional skills necessary to have connected, loving relationships. Without this mutuality and love, it's difficult for us to experience joy or be comfortable in our own skins. Men who are driven by deep, but unacknowledged, shame and anxiety often feel "entitled" to pass on that misery though violence against others, such as the women in their lives, their children, or even against women as a class. I'm recognizing here that male bonding is a driver of male supremacist ideology, and as such is central in sustaining and spreading what we now refer to as "toxic"—or poisonous, or lethal—masculinity.

Although toxic masculinity has entered colloquial use, it is still often misunderstood as saying that men are inherently bad, servants to their testosterone and delusions of grandeur. This is accurate if you believe that men are jerks by nature. I don't believe that— not for a second. Toxic masculinity, to my mind, is an aberration. It is not even normal in a statistical sense. Only a small minority of us might actually enact it—most men don't want to be seen as jerks—but toxic masculinity is normative in that most men would rather laugh with the guy bragging about how he wants to "hit that" or calling the girl a fat hoe than risk disrupting that privilege. So, most men are not jerks, but few men are willing to tell the jerks to knock it off.

Toxic masculinity requires men to position themselves in relation to its challenge; it is a gauntlet thrown down that asks us, "Which side are you on? Are you a man or not? Will you align yourselves with the ideology of male supremacy? Or are you willing to risk ostracism, ridicule, and potential violence by allying yourself with women, you pussy-whipped pantywaist?"

Toxic masculinity legitimizes the subordination of women to men and pins their manhood on men, demonstrating that they hold bros above women, that women are possessions, commodities, and currency. It feels natural, almost, because it's so reinforced in history, institutions, culture, and daily life. This norm of masculinity is a barrier to men taking accountability for the harm we cause. Male bonding happens when men agree to pretend that toxic masculinity is true, or okay, or inevitable, or natural, or tolerable with one another.

I have been running educational groups for men who buy sex for decades. When I am describing male bonding to these men, I say that it means that the biggest jerk in the room sets the norm—not the most thoughtful guy, the most interesting, the most engaged. Often, this dynamic will play out in the group itself. The biggest jerk will say something sexist, and the rest of the men will either agree or sit silently. Occasionally, someone steps up to interrupt the oppressive comment—but usually no one does, or, if they say anything at all, it is to me after class when they confide that they "didn't really agree with that guy." It is too scary to say it in the moment and risk betraying the male bond.

Just a few months ago, I was talking to one of my groups about intimate partner violence and, more specifically, about intimate partner sexual assault. Men who buy sex are more likely to commit intimate partner violence and sexual assault than those who do not buy sex. (These activities are enmeshed in ways that may not be immediately obvious, but the data is conclusive. From my experience, this has to do with shame and fears around vulnerability.) I was explaining to these men how, historically, women were considered the chattel property of their husbands under English common law. I went on to explain that, up until forty or so years ago, in most of the U.S., a man could legally rape his wife. On cue, one of the men quipped, "I call them the good ol' days."

There it was. The biggest jerk in the room had thrown down the gauntlet. I stepped back and watched the others position themselves in relation to the challenge. Some laughed and nodded defiantly. Some shook their heads as if to disagree but chuckled performatively under their breath, hedging their bets so they would not appear to the others to be a traitor to their sex class, a "pussy" or a "fag." Some stared at the floor, refusing to make eye contact. Some looked at me in anticipation of a response. I waited.

Finally, when it seemed clear that no one was going to interrupt, I asked, "Really? Is no one going to respond to [Biggest Jerk]? All of you think that it is okay for you to rape your wife?" There was another long and awkward pause, but then a man finally muttered quietly, looking down, "No, I don't agree. It's not okay to rape your wife." A few others nodded their assent.

Okay, obviously, this grudging response (and only when pressed) is unacceptable. Men need to step up and speak out against men's violence. I know speaking up is easier said than done because it has been so hard for me to learn to do it. As a teenager and into my early twenties, I played the male bonding game. It was the way I related to most men. Looking back, I was terrified of other men's judgment, ridicule, ostracism, and potential violence against me. I would participate, or laugh, or silently nod in agreement when some jerk spouted off in the locker room or school hallway—and later, at work or at the bar. I'd talk with friends in high school about "working a yes" out of a girl and "getting women drunk" so they could have sex, and then, at home, my sister would tell me about the sexual assault she experienced. I felt conflicted and afraid whenever I tried to reconcile those two realities.

My family was typical, too, in the way that we talked about sex. With my father, it was one terse mention in a car ride when I was ten or eleven years old. He said, "If you are going to kill someone, you put a silencer on the gun, and if you have sex, you wear a rubber." That was it—and my dad was a physician. My mother tried to talk to me, but it was too awkward for me. Looking back, I can understand that she really saw me; she knew I was a tender-hearted and sensitive, sweet human being, not the tough guy I was so desperate to become. I had to turn away from her during this time because tenderness is anathema to a "real" man. I now see that all of this sad bullshit is far from harmless, and that, in fact, a part of me died each time I participated in these types of behaviors. When I sold out my sister, I sold out myself. When I cut off from my mother, I cut off from myself. Toxic masculinity drives rape culture, to be sure, but when I say it wrecks lives, I mean all of our lives.

A growing number of men and boys are tired of this outdated mode of being and are finding the courage to explore alternative expressions of connection based on mutuality, love, respect, empathy, and compassion rather than on dominance, fear, control, inequality, and unfeelingness. If you, like me, don't want the biggest jerk in the room, or the country, to set the norms for the rest of us, just know that I have your back.

Those late-night chats with my father continue to weave the fabric of who I am becoming. Just two talkative dudes, asking questions, breaking everything down, analyzing life.

I Got That from My Dad

Rayshawn Richardson

I'm standing in the kitchen with the soft serve ice cream cone I just bought from the truck downstairs. I'm about to start enjoying my cool summer treat when . . . I drop it. Of course. I start loudly complaining, whining, and basically throwing a tantrum. I'm sixteen, and it's not cute anymore. Just like that, I hear a "stop complaining and man up" from the adjacent room.

That's my dad.

I've heard "man up" from him many times before. This might sound like a harsh response to my ice cream sorrow; I believe that I know what he is trying to convey. He doesn't mean, "Bottle up your feelings," or anything like that. He means, "Clean up the ice cream and move on." My dad believes that being a man mainly means dealing with your consequences. He says that a man looks at what he's done and learns from it, even if it's a painful lesson, and has spent my life trying to teach that to me.

I love my dad, and I really look up to him. Even though I'm a freshman in college, I consider him my guide. I often think that he's my best friend and, honestly, he's a lot of people's best friend. He's the kind of person who can and will make friends with anyone. If we're standing in line at the Home Depot, he'll start a conversation that just won't end. If we're driving home and someone's on the side of the street, needing someone to jumpstart their car, there is no way we're driving by. My dad is stopping, jumpstarting the car, and making a new friend.

It drives my mom crazy.

I've noticed lately that I'm always getting stuck in conversations that go on and on. It's usually me asking too many questions, engaging other people, and soon I'm in the middle of something that veered away from small talk long ago. I guess I got that from my dad.

My father grew up as a little mixed-race kid on Long Island. His mom raised him and his siblings; they struggled financially. He loves telling me crazy stories of standing on the back of pickup trucks as he and his friends drove by suburban houses, swinging a baseball bat at mailboxes, trying to get them all. He was a troublemaker, which is hilarious because of how responsible he expected me to be throughout my childhood. He wants me to learn from his mistakes. He met my mom on the LIRR when he was eighteen and she was twenty-three, and they fell in love. That was the end of making trouble for no reason and the beginning of our family.

I have a younger sister, Gianna, who is three years old—fifteen years younger than I am. It's weird to be able to witness my parents raise her. I can picture myself at Gianna's age and almost get a live reenactment of how they must have raised me. (That said, I know she gets away with a lot more than I did. The younger sibling always gets an easier time, right?) Already, I can see my dad imparting the life lessons he taught me to Gianna, like being a truthful person. That's Dad's number one rule: Don't lie to me.

When I was younger, I used to constantly lie about walking the dog. "Yes, I'm telling you, I walked Wizard!" I'd claim. But my dad could always tell. "Why would you lie to me?" he'd say, looking so disappointed that I'd do that to him. A commitment to honesty lines up with his "face your consequences" life lesson, too. Just "man up" and tell the truth. When I disappointed him, he'd sit me down for one of our one-on-one conversations on the living room couch so we could hash it out. We'd go into these long back-and-forths, sometimes until 2 a.m. I look back on those talks and see them as shaping who I am—my character. Those late-night chats with my dad continue to weave the fabric of who I am becoming. Just two talkative dudes, asking questions, breaking everything down, analyzing life. For instance, telling the truth is a simple, obvious virtue, but how he stressed it to me has really stuck. I'm always asking myself, *How can I be a more honest person?*

Everything's an opportunity for a lesson, according to my dad. These days, his message is, "Going to college *is* your job." He means that I don't need to worry about having a part-time job or earning pocket money while I'm in school. He's always helped me with school and been clear about his expectations for me. When I didn't focus, or did dumb stuff, or got in trouble, he'd say, "You're going in there to work." If I screwed up, he made me face my punishment and encouraged me when he saw I was doing better. He wasn't the kind of dad who complained to the teacher to give me a break.

I know how badly my dad wants me to graduate from college. I see it in the way he looks at me and hear it in the way he talks to me. "Just go in there and get your A's," he says. And I'm going to. For me, yeah, but also for him.

I couldn't let you walk past
without me saying something.

Man on the Street: A Monologue

Tariq Crabbe

This monologue was performed as part of Seeing Rape, *an original play devised and performed at John Jay College of Criminal Justice in New York City in May of 2018. I was a student at the time, working a full-time job in the Financial District and commuting to and from Sayreville, New Jersey every day. Growing up as the youngest of six kids, I didn't have the muscles (or looks in general, in my opinion) to get the ladies, so I did the best I could to use my own charm and be funny with it. I wrote this monologue in about thirty to forty minutes. It flowed.*

Yo! Yo, blue shirt! Yo! Blue shirt!

Excuse me, miss! I see you over there, you lookin' mad good today.

Yeah, how you doin', ma? Yeah you! What's up, beautiful!

Oh, you're married? Well, that's cool! We can all be friends!

Come over here, let me holla at you for a second? What's your name?

Damn, that's a sexy name.

Oh, your man thinks so too? Oh, wow, hahaha, you shot out, mama! Good thing I ain't gay, cuz I ain't tryin' to talk to your man, I'm tryin' to see what's up with you.

I'm just sayin', I'm just sayin', can I talk to you real quick?

I just want to say hi and get to know you a little better. Oh, wait a minute, what kind of phone is that? Is that the new Galaxy Note? Dang, this phone is hot. It would look so much better if my number was in there.

I know you got a man, but what that got to do with me? I'm talkin' to you right now, not him.

Hold up hold up hold up! Don't walk away, I was just playin'. I'm sorry. I just want to be your friend!

Oh, you already have enough friends? Well, none of your friends are like me, mama. One more won't hurt!

I don't have many friends, and the friends I do have, they all wack as shit. None of them are as stunning as you, sexy.

Oh, is that a smile I see?

Ah, so if I made you smile, I guess that means we are friends now!

No?

Okay, well, I'll keep being friendly until you're my friend. And the way you're blushing right now, that isn't going to take very long, now is it?

Oh! So she *can* laugh? Can I keep making you laugh? You have such a pretty smile, and you smell so good. Where are you headed off to this evening?

Oh, that's cool. I'm sorry, I just—I just can't stop looking at you; your beauty is so powerful.

How powerful? Well, turn around and look, do you see that up there? That right there! You can't miss it. The sun going down. Do you know why it's going down?

No?

Because your beauty shines so bright, all you had to do was walk outside, now you puttin' the sun to shame.

Ah, you like that? Good, cuz I pulled that one out of thin air just to make you smile.

But, yeah, I ain't tryin' to come at you crazy or anything like that, I'm just tryin' to see what's good with you.

I couldn't let you walk past without me saying something.

Well, let me give you my math, so I can keep being your friend. My number? It's 347-555-0921.

I want to be the brave person you want me to be. I don't want to cry.

The Mother-Son Interview

Jackie and Che Luxenberg

CHE, AGE TWELVE: What was going through your head when you first saw me?

JACKIE, AGE THIRTY-FOUR: "Wow, now I'm responsible for another human being and shit just got real." I remember thinking that, just twenty-four hours ago, I was one body, and now there are two bodies—and one body just came out of me. I thought, "How am I gonna do this?" It was exciting and amazing.

CHE: What have been the hardest moments with me growing up so far?

JACKIE: Holding onto my values. Like wanting to raise you my way and having to fight for that right. I don't do things the way the majority of moms do, so just holding on to what I think is right has been a challenge—but worth it.

CHE: Do you feel like you can cry in front of me?

JACKIE: I cry a lot. I'm sensitive. I think the last time I cried was probably last week. I can cry in front of my friends. You need to cry—it's bad for your body to hold in your emotions. Do I feel like I can cry in front of you? I *have* cried in front of you. I don't *like* to cry in front of you because I don't want you to worry.

CHE: **Do you see yourself in me?**

JACKIE: I do. We have the same brains. I say that to you all the time. The way that I see myself in you most is your willingness to try new things and be adventurous. You don't hold back, you just go for it, whatever it is, and I was like that when I was a kid. I hope you always have that and never lose it. I love that about you.

CHE: **Who was the biggest influence on your life?**

JACKIE: My grandmother. Abuela.

CHE: **What's your favorite thing about me?**

JACKIE: Your heart. How you're such a gentleman and take care of me and just what a good, kind person you are. And how you take care of yourself and you make good decisions.

JACKIE: **It's my turn to ask you questions. What are your biggest hopes for the future?**

CHE: That I make good friends who care deeply about me. That I get a girlfriend. That my business is successful. That my mom's business is successful. That my grandparents live for a long time. That I graduate from culinary school. That I travel to go to different culinary schools to learn different methods. That I travel the world with you.

JACKIE: **What's your favorite thing about me?**

Che: You've shown me that money isn't everything, and the moments you spend with your loved ones and the memories you make are what make life enjoyable.

JACKIE: Describe the last time you cried.

CHE: Well, I cried about you and Omar, because you guys kept on breaking up and getting back together, and it was confusing the hell out of me. You guys just break up and, in the end, you're always the one who gets hurt. I don't see him crying. I don't see him deeply hurt. If you guys are fighting, he thinks he's right, even though he's not. It breaks my heart to see you cry. But when I cry over you two fighting, it's not all out of sadness—a lot of it is being annoyed that the same old stuff is happening again.

JACKIE: Do you feel like you can cry in front of me?

CHE: Yeah, but I don't like to for the same reason you don't like to in front of me. It makes you all worried and I don't want you to worry. I want to be the brave person you want me to be. I don't want to cry. I really like that you taught me crying is a natural process. When you bottle all that emotion in, it can turn into sicknesses in your body and viruses—so let it out.

JACKIE: Do you feel like you can cry in front of your friends?

CHE: Currently, not really. They're too young to really understand and don't even really know me, they don't know my life outside of school. They're not like you; they don't know how to make the problem better.

JACKIE: In school, is there ever a time when you feel like crying?
CHE: Yes. When the teacher makes me feel like I'm not a smart person.

JACKIE: Here's a change of subject: do you know what porn is? Be honest.
CHE: Sadly, we have a ghetto person in my school, so how could I not?

JACKIE: What is a "ghetto person"?
CHE: A person who says inappropriate things out loud, not caring if the teacher's there. Yes, I know what porn is. But do I look it up on the Internet? No, I don't.

JACKIE: What are your thoughts about virginity?
CHE: Someone loses it because they're attracted to a person. They do what they need to do because they love somebody or something like that. I don't know exactly how it works because I'm twelve years old, but to me, it comes up when someone likes someone else and you can lose it or you can still have it. I don't get what the big difference is whether you have it or not, but I'm pretty sure I want to still have it at my age. I think [sex] is something if you want to have a kid or a family—it's serious. I don't think it's something to mess around with.

JACKIE: Is there anything too serious to joke about?

CHE: Yeah—there's a reason why I'm not friends with certain people, 'cause they make jokes where I'm just like, "Dude, that's so uncool." This boy I know tells jokes that are either extremely pervy, weird, or just disgusting. He's trying to get attention, and it's so hard to be around—for me, at least. I'm into jokes, but some people just take it to a whole other level where it's not even funny. It's just uncomfortable.

JACKIE: Give me topics that you think are too serious to be joked about.

CHE: Some people make fun of people being gay. Being like, "Bro, get off of me, that's gay" is a little stupid, but it's normal. Not even normal, I guess, but not that bad. They're just messing around. But you can take joking way too far. Same with talking about people's body parts—that can be taken way too far.

JACKIE: What are you most afraid of?

CHE: I'm afraid of not passing my grades. I try to use fear as a tool to push harder and farther and higher. I'm not saying that I'm so afraid of getting an 85, but I use that fear to, like, push myself to a 95, like I did in social studies.

JACKIE: Can you talk about your feelings with your friends?

CHE: I guess I can talk about my feelings when I'm

sad or something sucks, but I don't think it's taken into much consideration. I know my friends will listen, but they won't think, "Oh, he's feeling down—we should try to lift him up." It's just a waste of my breath, and then they maybe won't want to talk to me because they think I'm in some weird bad mood.

JACKIE: How do you treat your guy friends?

CHE: With respect, so they respect me. And with kindness and generosity and loyalty—a sense that I have their back in a fight or that they could lean on me.

JACKIE: How do you want to treat girls and women?

CHE: With kindness and respect, and to make them feel good about themselves because I feel like that is important to women.

JACKIE: Talk to me more about that.

CHE: When I grow up and get a girlfriend? Or just in general?

JACKIE: Just in general.

CHE: I want to be myself around a girl, you know. I don't want to be this other person. If they don't like who I am, then fine—I'm sure there are other women who will like who I am.

JACKIE: Do you know what rape is?

Che: Yeah.

JACKIE: Do you know what harassment is?

CHE: Yeah. It's not as bad as rape, it's like if some- one's calling you over and over again and you're like, "Stop!" or even like a company calling you over and over again.

JACKIE: It's talking to someone sexually or touch- ing them inappropriately when they said stop.

CHE: Oh, yeah, I know what that is.

JACKIE: How can you make sure you're not involved in these things?

CHE: I'm not fully into sex yet, so that's really how I just stay out of [rape and harassment]. If any- thing were to happen, you know, you ask first or something like that. You don't make a move out of nowhere.

JACKIE: How can I support you in this, as a parent?

CHE: I don't know. You're not going to hold up a sign that says, "Go Che! You got this, buddy!" But don't be weird about it—I don't know.

JACKIE: Next question. Do you think boys and girls can just be friends?

CHE: Yeah, it's easy. I have girls that are friends. Do *you* think boys and girls can be friends?

JACKIE: Yes, *but* I think having friends of the

opposite sex changes a bit when you're in a relationship and your boyfriend has nothing but girlfriends. I think there should be boundaries. Who wants to hook up more, boys or girls?

CHE: I mean all I hear about is boys talking about wanting to hook up with girls, so I'm guessing boys. Mostly the boys are playing "Smash or Pass" and stuff like that.

JACKIE: **What does it mean to you to be a man?**

CHE: It means "protect the ones that mean a lot to you." If you have a girlfriend or something, always be a gentleman. I don't mean that in a sexist way— like, women can take care of themselves, too—but I mean always walk on the right side, escort them to the safest way, or if it's raining or cold, give them your coat. To protect or comfort someone gives me enjoyment. Like, when I build a campfire for you, you're always like, "Che, sit down and watch it," but I get enjoyment out of your enjoyment—so I think that's what it means to be a man.

JACKIE: **Hmmm, for me, a man is someone that is strong, a protector, a provider, admits when he's wrong, learns from his mistakes, and isn't afraid to show his heart, emotion, or vulnerability. Someone who's willing to put in the work and living his full potential this lifetime. A man is someone who is able to express his emotions and stand by his values and thought** process in a raw way without putting anyone else down, and someone who holds space for the person he loves. And, okay, last question: What do you wish we could talk about that we don't talk about enough?

CHE: We talk about pretty much everything together.

JACKIE: I know we do. But what don't we talk about *enough*?

CHE: Video games.

Sex isn't making love. No, in our era of Pornhub and cam girls, sex is something completely fake, and forced, and unfair, and never really pleasurable for the girl.

That Girl

Priyanka Voruganti

"**H**e just sent me another one." Cara opens the Snapchat and tilts the screen towards me.

Tell me how big it is

"My fucking God, he's so—" I say.

"What do I say?" She jumps off the bed and looks in the mirror. She starts to lift her shirt off of her head.

"Be like, 'Wait, dude, can you send it again? I couldn't see anything.'"

"Stop. I don't want him to be like sad or something. I don't want to be mean."

I watch her take a photo of her tits. She's half turned away from the mirror, her ass is pointed towards the camera, and she's smiling a little. It's not really a smile though. It's more of a smirk. Like something porn stars do. That sort of "come over here" face. And all I can think about is how terribly fucking tragic my role is in all of this. The friend of the friend who fucks the dudes. The one who doesn't. The one who watches the Snapchats unfold but isn't sending or receiving. I look at her body. I mean, I *really* stare at it.

She takes another photo, this one with her vagina sort of in it. It's shaven and it's white and it reminds me of Venus. I feel like throwing up and taking a shower and dying. Because either you know how to do these things, or you don't, and there is no in-between.

You're either the one taking the photos or you're the one sitting on the bed, watching, wishing your body looked like your friend Cara's. I think about how I've never sent a nude and how I want to and how I wish someone would be waiting, at the edge of their bed, for days, cock in hand and forehead sweaty, waiting to open a Snapchat from me. I think about how I want to be desired.

Just then Cara looks at me and laughs, embarrassed. She says, "I love that I can do this in front of you. This is why you're my best friend."

But there is a secret to all of this. A sort of cheat sheet to nude-taking. You've got to be hot. That's just a given. Contort that body, suck in, tits out. But, more than that, you have to look fuckable. No one thinks a girl in a lion stance with a huge fat dildo on is sexy. You can't be weird or unique or funny. To allow yourself to be the object, you need to have a sort of innocence in your eyes, a little hint of submissiveness in your pout. You'll send the photos that he'll jerk off to, and he'll send some photos that'll inflate his ego. In no scenario are you, the girl, masturbating to any dicks.

Sorry.

I ask Cara if sending nudes feels like succumbing to the patriarchy.

"I wouldn't do it if I didn't want to. It's not like an obligation," she says. "It's just like, fun. I don't know. It's fun."

We lie on her bed, listening to Princess Nokia, laughing at Max's small penis.

And then, something changes. From Max: "Let me fuck you until you cry." We turn the music off. We're not laughing anymore. Max says he wants to fuck her doggy-style, wants to double penetrate her, wants to make her bleed.

Suddenly I'm not so jealous anymore. *Is that what Max thinks sex is? Slaying Cara's pussy, fully annihilating her vagina? Is that what would get him off? To see his sort-of-fuck-buddy crying, bloody and gross, laying on the floor, a body for him to pound into?*

"He watches, like, *way* too much porn," Cara says. She tries to laugh. I stare at her, willing her to be real.

"But does he?" I counter. "I mean, compared to most other boys, I feel like he's not so different."

She doesn't answer.

And then she stands up again and moves to the other side of the room, probably to hide her response from me. She says something like, "You can do whatever you want to me, baby," or, "I'm yours." She takes some more photos.

There's something so addictive about being objectified, taking these photos, getting verification from a guy that you're hot, you're sexy, you're beautiful, you're *worth* it. That's what I craved. Being *that* girl. The white, blonde, bombshell porn star—an ideal, an angel, a sex goddess. Because if you're not *that* girl, it sometimes feels like you're not *any* girl. You're not wanted. I mean, not really. Because these guys, they're watching hours of this shit, seeing *those* girls and guys like them get it on, violently, and then they want exactly that. So, the standards of sexiness for us girls are raised. These guys want the IRL version of the digital. And if your pixels don't exactly sum up to some sort of Riley Reid look-alike, fuck off.

Watching porn alters the way these guys, and us girls, view sex as a whole. Sex isn't making love. No, in our era of Pornhub and cam girls, sex is something completely fake, and forced, and unfair, and never really pleasurable for the girl. And I don't necessarily mean actual sex, but more so the concept of it. The way these young boys, upwards of ten years old, who take their cues from porn are thinking about sex is just completely wrong and delusional. They're ill-informed. They ingest gigabytes and terabytes of this fantastical, fabricated, destructive content and take the information they're getting as authentic sex ed. And then these girls, thinking sex involves a performance of exactly how it's depicted in porn, end up saying tragic goodbyes to their hopes and dreams of ever being able to truly enjoy sex. They see porn stars faking millions and trillions of orgasms and learn to mimic their "ahs," their "oohs," and their "give me more's." I think girls learn to view pleasure as a myth.

Meanwhile, Cara falls back on the bed, exhausted. Does she feel used? Does she feel fucked over, fucked with, fucked too much and too hard? No, she's satisfied. She's proud. She knows she has something I don't. She's *that* girl.

But these virtual flirtations, these online versions

of courtship and sex, always follow the code of ethics that online porn has created. The trade of photos is the mode through which the misogynistic, contrived ideal of woman as sex object that makes ego and orgasm is upheld. And that's not to say that people *can't* break out of the standard and share nudes in a healthy or normal way, but it's definitely hard to. And you don't see it very often. I think seeing your friend Cara spend ten minutes trying to get a shot of her boobs where they look big, but you can't see that she's pushing them together, will always be hard to watch. I think seeing your friend Cara toy with the idea that her sort-of-fuck-buddy may have a rape fantasy will always be hard to watch. And I think seeing your friend Cara equivocate the beauty of her body based on the level of sexual response from Max, or some other boy, to a Snapchat that she sent will always be hard to watch.

So I don't. Now, I don't watch. I'm not going to be that girl, the one that sees this. It's too hard. So, I look away.

Patriarchy, like white supremacy, is bizarre and full of holes. It contradicts itself by infantilizing those it privileges, thanks to all that coddling and manipulation.

Patriarchal Norms

Anastasia Higginbotham

FATHER

Dad's car rolls into the driveway around suppertime. The garage door opens slowly, rumbling the whole house, and then closes. I hear the door open and close between the garage and basement, and Dad's footsteps as he passes by the laundry on the line and starts up the stairs to the main floor, coming nearer, nearer.

Inside the house, from the first rumble, my body registers: "Norm's home." (My dad liked to be called his real name, even by his kids.) I tune into the sounds of his return as if my life and worth depend on it. *Is the house clean enough? Is dinner ready enough? Is the table set enough? Are our grades good enough?! Did we wash our hands?! Have we left anything undone that might make him angry?!*

The way my body responds, you would think Bluebeard was back and here we all are, covered in blood, having gone into the one room he told us to stay out of, where all the bodies are buried! The most important and powerful member of the family is about to step through that door, and if he doesn't like what he saw, we're done for.

This is a scene for shaking my head at, to shake the mirage out of my mind.

Now forty-eight, in my own grown-up household, the inconsistencies of that nightly ritual are apparent. If the man is so powerful, why does he need to be protected from a half-set dinner table, a bunch of kids with A's and B's on their report cards, who didn't wash their hands (or worse, lied and said they had), and a wife who hasn't finished making dinner yet because she just got back from grocery shopping and a million other errands? If that's all it takes to set him off, let's get it over with.

But the child in me, the daughter I was, checks my bravado. She reminds me that the father of the house, and also the lover, must be shown that he is loved and adored always—otherwise he will scream at us, fall into depression and commit suicide, suffer a massive, stress-induced heart attack, or leave us for someone who makes him feel good all the time in the way we failed to do. I believed this—and still do, to a degree that's beyond my conscious reach.

It's a belief that also suggests the children and mother have not just the responsibility, but the power, to keep the father/lover alive. It presumes the man of the house has no will to live and no resilience of his own, no rootedness or authentic connection to his life, this wife, and this family for his own sake. Another mirage.

Patriarchy, like white supremacy, is bizarre and full of holes. It contradicts itself by infantilizing those it privileges, thanks to all that coddling and manipulation. Our beliefs about who is most worthy, bred into family and social structures, warp everyone. We play our parts out of habit until, by grace or catastrophe, we learn to see through the distortions.

I wish even one of us had had the guts to shout the truth way back then: "Dinner is not ready! Our hands are not washed! Our grades are *meh*! We prop you up be*cause* we can see your weakness and vulnerability, and we resent that you punish us for ours!"

Sometimes, my sibs and I *did* feel confident we'd made a happy home for Dad to come back to and the rumble of the garage door caused a fit of joy. "Let's pretend we're sleeping!" we'd yell, and he'd come through the door to find us all slumped over the table or flung out on the couch or splayed out on a rug. 'Cause what's funnier than that?

Other times, even with all of that tiptoeing around, there was hell to pay. B's *weren't* good enough, and Dad kicked our actual butts for showing up to the table with unwashed hands (the kick came when you walked past him to get to the bathroom once your fakery was exposed). He experienced bouts of depression and wanted to end it all when his mother was dying. And then, he did leave us to be with someone who made him feel more adored.

My intuitions were spot on! Yay me.

Even now, the fear of patriarchal disapproval throbs in my muscle memory. The click of my partner's key in the apartment door, coming home from work, breaches time and space. "Norm's home," I think, *in those words*. Questions and recrimination follow: "What have I left undone or never begun?

What state of disarray am I, my home, and my children in? What fault will he find with us?"

BROTHER

"When I have a son," Dad told Mom before any of us was conceived, "he will be named Abraham Amedeo"— after the two men my father admired most, my mom's father from Italy and his own grandfather from Syria, both gentle, nurturing men. Abraham was named first even though he came third, and the rest of us (all girls) were named to match, planets circling the sun. "His feet didn't touch the ground the first two years of his life!" Dad says. It's true, our brother was beloved and indulged by many of the girls and women in our family and neighborhood.

Our mom is the eldest of eight and had been meeting the demands of all of the members of her family, especially the favored males, since birth. No doubt, this left her with some resentment. My brother challenged her authority daily, in ways she found intolerable. "I should have hit him with a 2x4 every morning," Mom says of raising my brother.

In my childhood home, either parent could hit us. They held back with the girls but let loose on Abraham. He was physically hit more, but seeing my brother actually hit with the expectation of being "the son," I learned that favor affords more freedoms but zero protection. My father was the cherished only son in his childhood home, too, and the beatings he took were legendary.

Cut to my brother's life outside our childhood home, where his favored status was neutralized by appearing gay *and* ethnic. Once he started school, Abraham was targeted for existing outside of masculinity as well as outside of whiteness. Even worse (and so much better), he could dance and had the audacity to do so. The hostility aimed at him was constant. Much was implied, or said under the breath, or with a glance, or with laughter. A lot was overt. Some was violent.

BOYS

In grade school, I kicked boys a lot in self-defense and in play. I chased boys and they chased me, and it was thrilling and violent and playful and consensual— until the day Henry L. grabbed my foot mid-kick and pulled me right off my feet. My ass hit cement and my head hit the brick wall behind me, and that was it. I was done playing that game.

In sixth grade, a boy grabbed a handful of my butt and, without hesitation, I wheeled around and slapped him across the face the way I'd seen women do on TV. I believed this was my right. But he surprised me then by grabbing the top of my head and shoving down, crunching my neck bones in a way that hurt for a week.

After this, I rarely got physical with the boys who tricked, bullied, harassed, or coerced me in middle school, high school, and college. The few times I did block or retaliate against their aggression or teasing, they hurt me. They were always stronger. It seemed stupid (not as in pointless, but as in really not smart) to engage with boys physically. Safer to placate them in person while despising them off-site.

SONS

I'm part of a generation of parents who are not allowed to hit our kids.

My first son was eleven months old when he smacked me in the face for the first time. Instinctively, I took his entire fist between my teeth and was about to bite down when I stopped and remembered that he is a baby and I wasn't injured, just *super* pissed off.

A few years later, and stronger, my son kicked me in the chest. Once, he punched me in the nose. Consistently, he refused to cooperate in ways that demanded extreme physical and mental effort. When redirection and "using my words" failed, when three chances failed, when consequences and time-out failed, when screaming at him failed, I got very, very upset. Fully adrenalized, I have pinned him against a wall, pushed him to the floor, held him down, and growled in his little face in my effort to establish dominance. I have consistently overreacted *and* been ineffective in enforcing limits on both my sons' behavior, as well as controlling my own when I am hurt and disrespected.

Their father, meanwhile, has engaged in none of this aggression towards them or me. Violence does not occur to him, though he has been known to lecture, shame, or stomp around yelling. Yet, all along, our kids have responded more to his authority and limits. Since he's not an *abusive* man, I can only conclude that they shape up around him *because* he is a man.

And you bet I'm offended.

From the first smack, my son's challenge to my authority felt personal, even though I know I'm supposed to understand that it isn't. This has always sounded like perpetrator talk to me. *This isn't about you.* (Whack!) *Stop taking this personally.* (Whack!)

The misbehavior I was reining in when I exerted my authority was to keep them from being hit by cars, falling down stairs, hurting other people, or making me late for work and meetings. This was not some elbows-off-the-table-clean-up-your-toys-get-better-grades nonsense. This was about safety and respect—but even in my rational approach to discipline, my sons *somehow* understood they could (should) push past my "no." Male entitlement had soaked into their bodies; I didn't see when it happened, but it happened.

To stop hitting my children, I saw a therapist and kept a notebook called "The Journal of No More Hitting." On one of the pages, I wrote in huge block letters what's at stake for me when my children reject my limits by ignoring, laughing, running away, resisting, and fighting me (all typical childhood behaviors): "My no means nothing in this lifetime. Never has and never will. Causing Pain = I will *make* you stop."

But I was also in pain. And that is what made me stop.

US

I write and illustrate children's books about my own ordinary childhood injuries, from the perspective of the child. It's an effort to heal myself so I stop harming others. That's the whole reason I do it—any benefit to anyone else is gravy. My fourth book, *Not My Idea*, is about whiteness and white supremacy. I was able to make that book because of the many revelations that came with fully taking in my own power to end white supremacy—in my own mind and body, first, and everyplace else, next.

One revelation was about self-love and self-worth. What do my white sons learn if they see me hating myself as a white person or hating (rather than noticing and rooting out) my own racism? They learn that in order to be loved, they must choose between loving themselves or someone else, as if one group has to be the bad guy, undeserving. Being seen as a bad guy when you want to be good triggers defensiveness. Then the whole thing backfires.

Feeling loved and worthy is essential—no one grows or is redeemed without it.

Another revelation is that it doesn't matter what I feel. Listen to how James Baldwin said it:

> If it hurt you, that is not what's important. Everybody's hurt. What is important, what corrals you, what bullwhips you, what drives you, torments you, is that you must find some way of using this to connect you with everyone else alive. This is all you have to do it with. . . . You must understand that your pain is trivial except insofar as you can use it to connect

with other people's pain; and insofar as you can do that with your pain, you can be released from it, and then hopefully it works the other way around too; insofar as I can tell you what it is to suffer, perhaps I can help you to suffer less.

Why is it a relief to understand that my pain is trivial? Because it lets me quit thinking it's my job to stop being hurt by unjust systems and the ways people, including children, play them out. Injustice hurts. That fact alone connects me to every person who experiences the pain of injustice—including the pain of participating in injustice, as I have.

Baldwin concluded, "Then, you make—oh, fifteen years later, several thousand drinks later, two or three divorces, God knows how many broken friendships and an exile of one kind or another—some kind of breakthrough, which is your first articulation of who you are: that is to say, your first articulation of who you suspect we all are."

To perpetuate patriarchy is to suffer in it. To defend the practices of white supremacy is to kill off one's own intuitive yearning toward love and justice, which the soul needs to survive. What I hear in the triviality of my pain is that oppression is rough. Everyone needs to be loved through it and liberated *up out of it*. Everyone. So, I'm trying to tune into liberation (my own and everyone else's) as if my life and worth depend on it. Because I suspect that they do.

So, I ask you, Mom, does it matter whether we know how to handle this stuff by now?

Feminist Mom Raising Sons: A Correspondence

Jennifer and Skuli Baumgardner

JENNIFER, AGE FORTY-NINE:

When you were little, Skuli, part of my job was traveling the country talking about feminism on campuses and conferences. People would often marvel that Amy [Richards, my *Manifesta* and *Grassroots* co-author] and I each had sons—as if it wasn't a fifty-fifty chance that we would. Or maybe the thinking was that ideally feminists were "blessed" with daughters. Sometimes these people would say that we—as outspoken feminist activists—were the right people to have sons, because we would raise good men.

The idea that feminists *should* raise sons always struck me as flattering and potentially true—but also wishful thinking. During Q and A's, people would often ask what I did that was different than the putative, non-feminist moms, but I couldn't come up with much. You were drawn to guns and weapons as a toddler, and I certainly let you play with them. At fourteen, you still like to do "live action" role play in your room with a stash of wooden swords, plastic knives, and guns cast off from Halloween costumes. I didn't push you toward gender-neutral colors, toys, or friendships. We didn't read *Heather Has Two Mommies* or even *Free to Be . . . You and Me.*

Two elements of my parenting do stand out to me,

though, and I wonder what *you* think about them. First, you *de facto* did not see gender roles around division of labor when you were little, because your father and I weren't together. When you were with me, you saw me working, cooking, doing the dishes, paying the bills, driving the car, caring for you, and managing your schedule. When you were with your dad, you saw him cooking, working, taking care of you, and managing the details of his apartment himself. Your dad taught you to play guitar and I was the one who put together the Ikea furniture and changed the light bulbs.

The second element relates more directly to sex, sexuality, safety, and development. Because of what I do for work, you were openly exposed to spaces and ideas from which kids are shielded. You've been to more than one abortion clinic in your life, since I often speak at them because I made a documentary about abortion, and because our good friend Merle Hoffman owns one of the largest clinics in America. We've talked about how I had an abortion after you and your brother were born, too. "Abortion rights" isn't siloed in political theory or opinion pages or slogans for you—it relates to your real life.

The other issue that I exposed you to early is the subject of my second documentary: sexual assault. I took you to see *SLUT: The Play* when you were ten years old and *Now That We're Men* when you were eleven. A piece of me worried that you were too young, but I also know many people who were raped in junior high and early high school. Over the years, we've talked a lot about rape—not because I want to freak you out. I have tried to connect myself honestly to the "issues" that I want you to think about, and to share with you the reality of my life. My hope is that you then feel safe telling me what is *really* happening in your life. Especially now that you are about to enter high school and, I think, be exposed to more mature socializing.

SKULI, AGE FOURTEEN

If I could describe your parenting in one word, it would be "desensitizing." I want to clarify, I don't mean that in a negative way. You did all a feminist mother should do to try and produce a well-rounded person. Desensitizing refers to the plays I was brought to (like *SLUT*), the concepts I was told about, and the books I had read to me (most boys I know didn't read *Are You There God? It's Me, Margaret* with their moms in sixth grade). I knew what words like "gay," "rape," or "anal sex" meant before most of my five-year-old peers. I watched mature movies like *Indiana Jones and the Temple of Doom* (which you showed me) and the *South Park* movie (Dad's idea, that one) when I was in kindergarten.

At Mom's house, I could say anything I wanted. At Dad's house, I could do anything I wanted. Most people would hear that and think that I'm probably screwed up now, right? Giving children too much freedom can result in two things, in my opinion: Being a brat or being self-reliant. I hate saying things like this, but I consider myself fairly self-reliant.

I often think about how I'm going to raise my kids. I want them to be like me when I was their age, but that involved my parents splitting before I could speak, which I don't want for them. One thing I would love for you to explain to me is what kind of person you wanted me to be as I was growing up.

JENNIFER: Oh, boy, Skuli. What kind of person did I want you to be? Definitely self-reliant, kind, perceptive, curious. I was very relieved when your little brother Magnus was born and you were so sweet with him. You never left him out or acted annoyed when he wanted to be with you; you took seriously the impact you had on his self-image and his little life. You've always been remarkably patient with younger kids, and I'm very impressed by that. I also felt like Magnus allowed you to connect to family without always feeling like you were being pulled between me and your dad. You two have a good bond—at a minimum, watching you two together has been very healing for me and all of the guilt I feel complicating your life by my choices.

When you were very little, I just wanted you to grow and develop and for me to be able to get you the support you needed to deal with the reality that your parents were "in conflict." Not all separated families have this issue, but Dad and I didn't have the same rules, values, or approach to parenting. Now that you, like, shave and are suddenly taller than me, I want you to be the kind of person who can talk to girls as friends, who knows how to be your "true" self and stay in touch with what you think and feel, regardless of who you're interacting with. This is unrealistic, perhaps. Maybe growing up is about trying on identities and figuring out how to get people to like you.

I can laugh about it now, but I felt very insecure as a teenager—as we've discussed. I didn't feel like what was special about me was necessarily valued at my junior high and high school in 1980s Fargo, North Dakota. I didn't try to be part of the norm at my school—the norm being football, hockey, drinking, and date rape. I was into fashion, theater, and, basically, talking about abortion rights—not a recipe for popularity. Still, I wanted to be liked and for guys to find me beautiful. I thought cheerleaders were idiots, but I was envious of them, too—especially the hockey cheerleaders who did all of their jumps on ice, in skates.

In retrospect, I see that my wobbly self-esteem meant that I wasn't genuine as a teenager. I had two serious boyfriends in high school whom I loved, but I felt too vulnerable to be vulnerable with them and instead acted sort of hostile and sarcastic. (Michael might say I still have a bit of this instinct.) I had *tons* of nervousness about sex and kissing—fear of doing it wrong, of being bad at it, of not being attractive enough, of being pushed to go too far—but I couldn't really articulate my questions or my boundaries. Sexual interactions, especially unwanted attention, rendered me tongue-tied. I think one of the reasons I was so drawn to feminism once I got to college and beyond is because I felt permission to express more of who I was inside. That need to be more real and still be valued was also what drew me to theater and music.

As you've matured, I have thought a lot about me and my sisters' early sexual experiences, some of which were negative-to-traumatic. My inability to communicate what I was feeling, even if it was confusion, contributed to bad experiences for me. I presumed, too, that guys wanted sex and if you wanted to spend time with them, you had to deal with being groped or worse. On the other hand, girls enforced some of the cruelest behaviors: spreading rumors about other girls, or knocking them down for trivial reasons. Basically, high school didn't feel safe.

What I want for you is to understand that those sinister teenage social vortexes are bullshit and you shouldn't be afraid to opt out. I want you to be stronger than I was. My biggest fear is that you will be part of something that hurts you or someone else in a life-changing way, and that it will happen almost by accident, because there are all of these unspoken rules about masculinity and femininity and sex and coolness and invulnerability that intertwine with other very real feelings of needing to be accepted and to find love and validation.

SKULI: For starters, I can assure you that no sex, abuse, coolness, or masculinity has happened or will happen during my time at middle school. As I've said to you before, I believe that my particular middle school has slowed the social development of the students inhabiting it, including me. I don't mean that we are all incapable of speaking or making eye contact, but people in my grade (eighth) have *just* started dating. By contrast, I've heard stories of people at other schools having sex for the first time at thirteen. Separate of my socially backward schooling, I'm sure that your biggest fear won't be realized. You've helped me gain the confidence I need to express what I feel and be considerate to what others feel.

JENNIFER: I like that your school is nerdy. New York is a fast-paced town.

SKULI: Sure, but slowed development is something else entirely. The problem that presents is that social drama, rumors, etc. happen rarely and, as such, when they do happen, people scramble for a place in the story. I think that this school has not prepared me for the social kerfuffles of high school. So, I ask you, Mom, does it matter whether we know how to handle this stuff by now?

JENNIFER: Hmmm. It depends on what you mean by "handle." I think it's healthy that your school put the brakes on flirtation and sexting and that there are policies (whether or not they are always abided) restricting students from having social media accounts. You are getting to have a real childhood. On the other hand, high school might be a bit of a rude awakening if you're suddenly faced with kids sharing nudes and don't know what your personal "policy" is. Let's start figuring out what your policy is going to be, so you have at least given it thought.

Speaking of nudes: I wanted to ask you about porn. I know you watch it and I don't really have a problem with that. I do have a problem, though, with it passing for some sort of sex education. I see it as showbiz, designed to turn a person on, but totally a performance (often kind of tacky and gross, for my tastes) and *really far* from good sex. What I slowly learned over time is that good sex involves some vulnerability and intimacy, and is closer to a deep and honest conversation than it is to a pile-driving orifice slam. (Thank God.)

SKULI: I'm not sure that my school's policy is what kept me from social media. I think that Instagram and Snapchat have just always been little more than ways to embarrass yourself, at least for kids my age. I agree that the policy put the brakes on flirtation and sexting, and that's a good thing, but it doesn't remove us from all of those things. The culture at my school made two types of kids: the ones that went on to "flirtation and sexting" despite the school's efforts, and the ones who never got that social muscle working. The rude awakening will really get them. I know my "policy" very well; if someone sends me a nude, I delete it. I'm not very worried that I will be in a social situation and not know what to do, and you shouldn't be either.

I think "pile-driving orifice slam" is a great description of porn. It combines the mindless pyrotechnic fun of a wrestling match with the detached euphoria of getting to slam an orifice. I have a very clear line drawn in my head between the emotionless fun that is porn, and actual relationships and feelings. I'd like to know if you are cautioning me about porn and high school for safety's sake, or because you think I might not be ready for them. My image of myself might be clouded by overconfidence, so I would love to know.

JENNIFER: Well, your step-dad and I have talked about this a bit. I'm not really worried about you exactly, but you will be exposed to new social situations in high school, and certainly you will have more freedom. I could imagine being at a party or witnessing some new interaction being confusing for you merely because you haven't experienced much peer pressure, intoxicants, and other things that can mar judgement. Also, perfectly normal kids do fucked-up things at your age, not because they are bad or stupid or evil, but because maybe they are immature, or lonely, or embarrassed not to, or misreading signals. A lot of sexual assault happens between the ages of thirteen and twenty-two. My need to be detailed with you about how common that is comes from my own experiences, and I don't think I'm being histrionic or overstating things.

Where I am much more ignorant than you, and therefore more likely to get the danger wrong, is online risks. You know to delete nudes and never forward them—good. You know (I assume?) not to take pictures of your penis and send them around as your calling card, even as a joke. But there are so many other pitfalls—even some with porn. If you download anything, if you end up on some underage site, if you see something you can't unsee. I know you are curious and that pornography is a natural part of that curiosity. I also want you to feel like your relationship with sex and masturbation is outside of my purview to edit or control you. The fact that you say you can distinguish between the emotionless fun of porn and what might be happening in real sex or relating is pretty persuasive to me. Basically, I want us to talk about these things, because they relate to much bigger issues around keeping you and other people safe from harm and safe from harming—which is another kind of trauma that will warp you.

Speaking of harming others: If you were accused of being involved in hurting or bullying someone, the worst thing I could do is defend you blindly. We would need to understand your part in it and be accountable to it. "Protecting" kids, especially boys or people who might have a certain kind of social privilege, from hard or shameful feelings, or from being called out, stunts their emotional—and even intellectual—growth.

SKULI: For a while I've had this vision that I would be able to expertly navigate the social gauntlet of high school and not fall victim to any of the common blunders. I've recently questioned that idea. Say I do end up refusing some "intoxicants"; will I get bullied? That is so far gone in my mind as something that could happen, yet I've never been to high school.

I have never worried about bullying before, as most bullying stories I've heard from friends are on social media. But what if I get talked into getting social media? That is what I'm worried about. I'm also concerned that I might be naiver on the subject than I previously thought. Sending dick pics as a "calling card" is so foreign to my world, but if you think it's worth mentioning then it's probably common.

JENNIFER: Even if I'm overstating the prevalence of dick pics, as a clueless Gen X parent, I'd rather we talked about it than not. One last thing—I know that my primo moments as your parent are unlikely to be *your* favorite moments, but an experience I loved, you mentioned earlier: when we went through the phase of reading Judy Blume books together before you went to bed. Judy Blume was my favorite author as a kid. Everything positive I learned about penises, I first learned from her. She had a character, Michael, introduce his penis, named Ralph, in a friendly way to his girlfriend before they had sex, her first time. (She's named Katherine, I think? I can't remember exactly—but Ralph is indelible! And now I'm married to someone named Michael. *Hmm. . . .*)

You and I read the funny ones, of course, like *Superfudge* and *Tales of a Fourth Grade Nothing*, but I especially loved reading *Are You There God? It's Me, Margaret* to you. It gave us a chance to normalize periods and changing girl bodies and a window into girls' experience of puberty just as you were about to enter into your own. You asked interesting questions and made comments that helped me further understand the brilliance of that book, as when you noticed that Margaret was so worried that she didn't have an adequate relationship to God because she didn't really have a religion, but she was the character who spoke to God the most in the book. So true! And something that I didn't really grasp as a kid, because I was so excited to read about bust exercises and first periods.

The reason those Judy Blume experiences are precious to me is that I think boys are socialized to be ignorant about girls' bodies in their human reality, and obsessed with girls' bodies in their unreal form (i.e. porn, air-brushing, et cetera). I think girls are socialized to be alienated from their bodies—taming their body hair, worrying about smells, giving orgasms without knowing how to get them, to name a few problems—and maybe we need to start talking about all of these things in mixed company, at any age, as if they are normal and human.

What did you think of those books and the kinds of conversations we had? What do you think of the one we are having now?

SKULI: *Are You There God? It's Me, Margaret* was definitely a learning experience. I would actually love to read it again now that I'm older. Those books are a great tool for teaching children about the nuances of other people. One of the moments from the book that I remember really affecting me was when Margaret's really confident friend cries after having her period. That moment holds so much relevancy to the teenage years that I'm going into, and the book has many more scenes like that. The other Judy Blume book we read about puberty, *Then Again, Maybe I Won't*, was weirder for me. From what I remember, the main character is coming to terms with all of these shameful teenage things like peeking into girls' windows, having wet dreams, and acting all tough around friends.

These moments are where the book diverted from reality for me. All the notions of toxic masculinity and being predatory or disrespectful to girls and how guys can't show emotion is really hammered into the reader and just boys in general. The problem is I don't really see those behaviors in my friends now. Sure, some of them might be creepy, sexist, or homophobic in secret, but that is not what they project. This archetype of a frat-bro-douchebag is not very common, in my experience. While I really appreciate the knowledge that reading those books provided me with, I wonder if they're sometimes based off of antiquated stereotypes about boys.

It's impossible to ponder masculinity and the factors that have made me the man I am without considering race. The two social constructs are desperately intertwined—codependent threads woven together and bound by necessity.

Many Rules to Learn

Justice Nnanna

Ike, meaning energy, is the essence of all things human, spiritual, animate, and inanimate. Ike was the first name given to me by my Igbo father. Later, I would be called by, and respond to, many other names—some more agreeable than others. "Boo-ka" by my baby brother. "Isa" or "Nnanna" by my relatives. "Grasshopper" by my godmother. "Justice" by my mother, and "My Good Boy" by my father. I suppose I had so many names because I meant so many things to the people who reared me. "Booka" when I played the leader, "Good Boy" when I played the follower, and "Grasshopper" when the Ike within my young body couldn't be contained and I played too much. It's Igbo belief that everything has its own unique energy, which must be acknowledged and given its due. A common maxim of this belief is the phrase *Ike di na awaja na awaja*, meaning, "Power runs in many channels."

If power runs in many channels, then the same must be assumed for energy. As a child, energy was an unacknowledged phenomenon—much like breathing and the absolute certainty to have more questions than answers about the world I witnessed around me. Energy was effortless. It was led by nothing more than the fact that it existed as a part of me.

Nothing concerned me much, except the attention I was given. As I aged and my life evolved, the complexities followed suit. Exponentially. Energy, which hadn't originally been gendered, was now something to be possessed and harnessed as a tool for success and, more importantly, survival. "The boy possesses a masculine energy," or, "He's got a feminine energy."

By the age of six, the period of free association and unfettered being had ended. Or, at least how I had known it. Unbeknownst to me, society was neither a blank slate waiting for my maturity to mold it, nor was it perfectly settled with all the world's issues addressed and settled in favor of fairness and justice. By first grade, I was being raised solely by my mother, a compassionate nurturer with emotional intelligence, a cutting survival instinct, and a keen awareness of the challenges she would face in her predicament. Presenting a facade of security, freedom, and happiness was manageable while her children were young—but the leaks in the dam were relentless, and she knew that, pretty soon, her sons would at least have to learn how to swim.

Circumstances had led my mother into the very position in which she so desperately aimed to avoid. The position she witnessed her mother struggle through, and the position her mother witnessed a generation before: a single black female, raising children alone. And worse, perhaps, my mother was a woman tasked with raising black boys into men. It's impossible to ponder masculinity and the factors that have made me the man I am without considering race. The two social constructs are desperately intertwined—codependent threads woven together and bound by necessity. The societal hierarchy is evident in the sequence of my classifier: "black man." First black, then man.

As with most constructs in a racialized society—masculinity for black men is governed by a whole different set of requirements then masculinity for other men. Societal expectations fluctuate depending on the richness of melanin. I went to a very multicultural elementary school in a suburb of Los Angeles. The majority of my closest friends were first-generation Americans with parents from Cuba, Mexico, Pakistan, Sierra Leone, and Iran. At ages six, seven, and eight, warning signs from the people who reared me became more frequent. *You're different than your white friends at school—if they get in trouble, it's okay; it's not okay for you to get into trouble.*

I began to understand what they were trying to convey when my second grade "girlfriend" severed ties with me after recounting that her "father was killed by a black man." She twiddled her glittered fingers, bit her bottom lip, and gazed wide-eyed at me for sympathy. She performed vulnerability, and I obliged by performing empathy. Hurt as I was by her break-up speech, I quickly assured her that I understood. I apologized for her loss, for that man that supposedly killed her father, and for my existence which seemed to be triggering her pain. In retrospect, this was early conditioning in teaching me that my existence, even as an eight-year-old, was something to apologize for. Regardless of our respective people's history, it was somehow my burden to apologize for the crimes of someone from my race. Shame disguised as humility—there are many rules to learn.

Now That We're Men, in all of its gruesome and accurate depictions of teenage masculinity, reminded me of the incredibly gentle nature of boys. Moving through life painfully insecure, eager to be liked, needing to be loved. Navigating through adolescence felt like constantly passing between moments of pure fantasy and stark reality. Playing Cowboys and Indians joyously for three hours, and then being told "niggers can't be cowboys." Getting accepted into my dream university, and then finding out it'll leave me a quarter-million dollars in debt at twenty-one. Being eight years in power, and then being blasted by a forty-five.

The fantastical moments were always born out of living unafraid of perception—effortless Ike. A group of teenagers drinking Slurpees, playing Pokémon, racing bikes top-speed through the Sepulveda Dam at magic hour. The neighbors converging in our living room every Friday night to celebrate the end of the work week by dancing like mad to Prince and Janet. *That's the way love goes.* The moments of stark realities, by contrast, were often when I realized that masculine performance was knocking, beckoning to be used as a tool to oppress.

Because I was being raised by a woman, eyes gazed harder on my Ike. Was I exhibiting "sissy" energy when I played kickball? Was I too soft? Did I still cry when I was upset, or had I matured appropriately to replace those feelings with anger and rage?

I remember first growing leg hair. I documented its length in bewildered amazement. The transformation from smooth limbs to slightly fuzzy ones was magic as good as I had ever seen. Preparing for school one day, I asked my mother if, when I lotioned my legs, I should spread the lotion down, with the grain of my leg hair, or against. She replied, "Spread it down, Justice; you want your legs to look nice and smooth." Smooth, huh? Well, shaving cream foam always looked fun when I'd catch my mom hastily shaving her legs while singing along to Zhané's "Hey Mr. D.J." before a night out with her friends, or in that Ben Stiller film *Heavyweights* when the cool fat kids compete at shaving balloons. If I wanted my legs to be nice and smooth, what better way than with mom's razor and some fun foam? Days later at school, some perceptive classmates noticed my patchy shave job. I was called *ladyboy* and teased mercilessly. After days of ridicule, I decided I'd lie and pretend that I hadn't shaved my legs "like women do"—my legs were just naturally smooth "in certain patches." Somehow an exploration of foam turned into a secret to be ashamed of, a deception to uphold. *Hide what you do if it'll make other people uncomfortable*—another rule to learn.

The burden of performed masculinity felt like a necessary component of maturing out of being a Good Boy and becoming a man. Masculinity for most of the men in my life evolved as a survival mechanism. When vulnerability and individuality are taken for

weakness, and weakness is seen as being incompat-
ible with survival, boys perform in ways that allow
them to hide their vulnerability and individuality.
Masked behind tough-guy aggression, behind misogyny, behind substances, behind apathy, eventually
creating such a calloused, protective layer that their
true self is unable to ever break through. The self-de-
stroying is itself the harbinger to the hurt you'll inflict
towards everyone else thereafter.

Growing up, I saw sensitive boys dissolve into
unrecognizable vessels as they struggled to main-
tain themselves under others' ridicule. I witnessed
this cruelty closely when my brother, at a young age,
expressed interest in cooking. Family members gave
shoddy looks to one another while my mom encouraged his culinary creations and indulged his curios-
ities. There were many rules to learn. But only she
could teach me that strength shows itself in many
forms—and none of them are gendered.

Regardless of the tragic roots behind toxic masculinity, there's no excusing the hurt, destruction, and
irreversible damage it causes every day. It is a global
brutality in which women and children experience
exponentially more harm than men do. Nonethe-
less, there is a need to revisit the factors that impact
boys' formative years and reevaluate the expectations
placed on boys as they transition into adulthood. *Now
That We're Men* cleverly places its characters in teen-
agehood—the exact moment when boys are typically
lost to manhood.

I no longer feel that necessity to perform masculinity

because I've accepted the undeniable truth that my time on Earth is best spent being myself, whatever that looks like. I no longer seek validation from people who are prejudiced or unwilling to see past fear to be themselves. Perhaps that self-development indicates that I've become as grown as one could ever hope to be. I watched *Now That We're Men* in wet-eyed wonderment when I realized that the boys depicted still believed in the falsity of "adulthood." They believed in the myth that they would one day become omniscient "adults" who have reached a point of complete contentment and actualization. They believed that we become men. I smirked, remembering that I once tightly held that belief. What I've come to learn is that, even with age and wisdom, we never reach absolute understanding and actualization. We never have to become "men." We are just boys grown tall.

I am, along with most of society, drawn to a certain stereotype. A stereotype that really hurt me, and that is more likely than not hurting you.

Reflections of a Queen

Louis J Levin

Ifirst came out in a high school assembly. It's one of those things that shocks me a little every time I say it, but at that moment it felt perfectly normal. I was ready. Having spent so long keeping up a front as that guy—cool, straight, normal—letting it all go was wonderful. In the weeks and months following, I began to explore parts of myself I'd always blocked off. I embraced my femininity, no longer worried about the assumptions people might make. I became more willing to stand up for what I believed in. More confident in who I was and what I wanted.

Coming out also meant I could now talk about—and have—sex. My goodness, how exciting! I'd spent all of puberty pretty much watching from the sidelines and did my best to make up for that as quickly as I could. I got Tinder—then Grindr, Chappy, and The League. It was, in part, a vanity project. I selected my most dashing photographs and made sure to mention my London roots (I had to flaunt my accent in some way or another!). I quickly learned that the world of online hookups can be rather barren, especially for people as picky as me. *He's too fat. And he needs acne cream. And, wow, the more I do this, the more superficial I become!* What caught me by surprise, however, was a common trend in people's bios. As I swiped, I noticed a lot of guys would brand themselves with a gender stereotype. They might say that they were "tough and strong," or that they "wouldn't strike you as gay." Some outright said "masculine," or "masc" for short. A few would specify the stereotypes they expected the men they fancied to embody. "No fem." "Only real guys." It made me uncomfortable.

I'd always struggled with the expression of my own gender. Growing up, I had been one of those boys who played with Barbies and dolls. The one who tried on his cousin's lurid pink dresses. The kind of guy you expect to be gay. And—rather annoyingly—I was. The fact that I fulfilled stereotypes of my sexuality bothered me. In a self-centered way, I wanted to buck the trend. In a more human way, I didn't want people to conclude that the assumptions they were making were universally accurate. At a certain point, I realized that being dishonest with myself was only going to leave me insecure, sad, and alone. So, out I came. But seeing those bios stirred something up. I'd always assumed the gender constructs that had left me so miserable were unique to the straight world. But it seemed that gays were busy reinforcing them, too.

It had taken me a long time to let go of the voices in my head. To stop caring what other people thought. To react with a smile and a laugh when someone shouted "faggots" at me and a boy holding hands on a bustling New York street. But, once I got there, it was liberating. I was liberated. I could do what I wanted, with who I wanted, whenever I wanted. I could love whomever I chose. Yet, this realization of the gendering of the gay world fractured that: I wasn't free after all. The constructs that I'd railed against were back to haunt me. I felt a newfound pressure to come across as more masculine. When a guy would comment on my fashion aspirations, I'd feel hurt. When another would say they hadn't known I was gay, I'd feel proud. I was backsliding quickly.

And, most difficult of all, I was aware of what I was doing. I'd lost a part of what I gained in coming out—that relaxed, happy, fuck-it vibe which had emerged so unexpectedly. In its place, the familiar self-consciousness started to appear. No, it didn't start to appear. I made it appear. I sought to hide from my own free will. I was choosing to change myself, to go against who I was. Yes, the social pressure was there, but I was a grown adult. In New York City. Immensely privileged, relatively thoughtful, I should have known better, been better. I had no excuses.

Then one day, something happened:

There is an air of uncertainty. Yes, our eyes had met in that tantalizing way, but I can't be quite sure. I stride forward. He does too. I seek his gaze out once more amongst the sea and then take a step closer, emboldened. His broad left shoulder turns ever so slightly, in time with the beat. I hesitate. We are close now, close enough to touch. I can make out the vivid blue veins rippling along his curled bicep. My attraction swells. Dancing my arm down, I brush his tensed thigh. Startled, he twists his head towards me.

I pause for a moment, leaving my hand lingering on the crisp acid-stained denim. He doesn't bat it away, but he doesn't look up either. I turn to a friend and try to act casual, bobbing along to the thumping bass. He gives off a cool, collected air I am deeply jealous of—and attracted to. He seems almost disinterested, looking me in the eye every now and then but not giving me a sign. Just as I am getting ready to call it a day, a right eyebrow rises and a smile eases across his face. I grin back.

Green eyes, thick scruffy hair, wide shoulders. That triangular shape enjoyed by celebrities and porn stars. There's something rough about him. Bushy eyebrows, the spots he's missed shaving, a rusted chain. His masculinity is overt without being overwhelming. I feel drawn to him. A real man.

We continue to dance, our eyes connecting every now and then. Atom by atom, the world around us begins to dissolve. It is just the two of us now. No judgment, no side eyes, no stares.

I push him back against the wall. He's not used to someone else taking control. My eyes find his. I lean in, our lips locking, his over mine. In the midst of the thronging mass, we find stillness.

My hand reaches up under his shirt, stroking soft, smooth skin. It inches down his stomach, his abs pulsing under my fingertips. I arrive at a waistband and push further. In a quick move, he spins us around and shoves me back so now I am up against the wall. He pushes hard, hard enough that I can't move my hand any further. He then chuckles, leans towards my right ear and whispers. "I don't go any further with queens like you." He pulls back— removing my hand in the process—turns on his heels, and dances into the moonlight.

That line has kept me up many a night. The rejection itself I got over relatively quickly—there aren't necessarily plenty of gay fish in the sea, but there are a fair few! What he said to me, however, didn't fade so easily. At first, it was because it hurt. It stabbed at an insecurity—my struggle to conform to gender expectations. I ran through the floral shirt I wore that evening and my funny, fluid dance moves. What had made him view me as effeminate? Over time, however, hurt moved to guilt. I'd been drawn to him specifically because he embodied the masculine. A hardened, manly façade that I found attractive. The same façade that I felt pressured to present. I was reinforcing gender stereotypes while simultaneously falling prey to them. I was part of the problem.

And the tricky thing is, I still am. Conceptual thinking is something I'm relatively good at. I've analyzed to oblivion my own attractions to—and applications of masculinity. I have thought about how much the endless fight for LGBTQ+ rights has been fought not by those who blend in, but by those who stand out. The "queens" of this world. I have gained a deeper understanding of just how impactful expectations of masculinity can be. The ways that people are influenced. The pressure they feel. And how they bend to it.

But theory can only go so far. Challenging the world around me is far easier than challenging myself. Changing who I am attracted to (and the extent to which I'm willing to compromise my beliefs in order to garner their affection) is incredibly difficult—as anyone who has struggled with their sexuality knows all too well. The heart wants what the heart wants. But the heart also wants what society taught it to want, and I don't know how to tell it otherwise. When presented with a hypermasculine guy, I can't help but feel a pull. And, I suspect, many straight men feel much the same, though perhaps in different ways. An attraction not to masculine people, but rather masculinity itself. A desire to be the "bro" of the school. A wish to be a seen as tough, as cool. In that sense, my yearning is utterly un-special. I am, along with most of society, drawn to a certain stereotype. A stereotype that really hurt me, and that is more likely than not hurting you.

So, what to do about it? How do we as individuals stop gender stereotypes from playing such subtle, significant roles in our lives? Can we reclaim our free will? Or are we so shaped by social expectations that we're simply past the point of no return?

There are a lot of questions, and I don't have definitive answers to any of them. But simply through questioning I've gained something. Not tangible change. No Hail Mary. Just a sense of self that I think is proving useful. A pause; a moment where I interrogate myself about my reasons for being attracted to someone. I might not have been able to shift the kinds of guys I find appealing, but I am more willing to challenge myself about it. All I can hope is that that is a good first step.

It's easy, I've learned, to point the finger. To look around and clock the infinite ways in which other people conform. To note just how harmful assimilation and blind reinforcement can be. But it is far harder to turn inwards. To challenge yourself. To think deeply about your own relationship to gender and its stereotypes. So perhaps, for now, the best answer I can share is just that: Ask yourself the questions.

Now, try putting yourself in Nick's position for a second: drunk as all hell, having the time of your life at a college party early in your freshman year, and a cute girl wants to get with you. What could go wrong?

Blackout

Willie Upbin

Ihave to admit, merely by talking to Nick for two minutes, it was hard to believe that he was involved in the Incident. He was a freshman, and I was a sophomore, but we had a couple classes together and saw each other at parties. Nick wasn't that kind of guy— he was too genuine, too righteous. There was just no way.

Nick and Ashley had been flirting with each other since the beginning of the semester. By October, some kind of hookup was inevitable. No one predicted that the Incident would occur, but after a few cups of Svedka and OJ, anything can happen. That's the problem, isn't it? The common mentality is that, if you drink enough, you just let the alcohol take over your brain, and that absolves you from any of your sins during the night ahead. Wake up, repeat.

A hookup at a frat party follows a well-worn path: a "conversation" riddled with base-level intellectual content because you can't hear a damn thing anyway (another red flag), roughly two to three minutes of close-quarters dancing (maybe more, maybe less—it depends on how awkward the dude is), a dance floor make-out, and if both parties click, the ordeal could take itself back to a dorm room. Now, try putting yourself in Nick's position for a second: drunk as all hell, having the time of your life at a college party early in your freshman year, and a cute girl wants to get with you. What could go wrong? That's what we think when we are in the moment—and therein lies the catalyst to the Incident.

When Nick woke up the next morning, he encountered a slew of profoundly disheartening texts on his iPhone notifications screen: "You fucking dick, how could you do this?" "You're disgusting." "Never talk to me again." You get the idea. Nick told friends he had no clue why he received any of these texts.

In a small school with a bunch of defined social cliques and a thriving Greek life, an Incident travels like wildfire. Not just like regular California forest fires, but like *Game of Thrones* Blackwater Bay wildfire. Gossip is like a game of telephone (yeah, that has definitely been said before, but it is accurate): each time the same story is told it gets distorted, just a tad, and soon terms like "rape" and "sexual assault" were used in the retelling multiple times. The story that reached Nick was that Ashley had been blackout-drunk, and she didn't remember hooking up with him at all. When she "blacked" in, he was having sex with her, and the rest is history. This version of the Incident differed from Nick's personal accounting, which was that the two engaged in a routine hookup that led to voluntary sex from both parties.

In the dangerous college hookup environment, Nick and Ashley's story (with little variation) is not uncommon. For college administrators and Title IX investigators charged with ensuring student safety and rights, these Incidents involving underage drinking and sex are almost comically (and tragically) impossible to resolve. How can we know who's right? Who's lying? Who do we blame? What is the punishment? How is the illegal drinking factored in to the testimony and punishments? Answering any of these questions provokes a dilemma: formally accusing someone of sexual violence (disrupting their life and education) and expelling them via extrajudicial proceedings, or protecting someone who has committed a significant crime because it's too hard to know for sure what happened that night. The students are affected, too, taking sides and spreading background details of the Incident. A subconscious anxiety that they could be embroiled in an Incident (some relating to Ashley, others to Nick) fuels the outrage.

The level of fragility around Incidents is like Kanye's mind before he drops an album—one minute everything is good, and, well, the next minute everything blows up like a neutrino bomb. Some Incidents like this stay insulated and don't leave the gossip realm. Yeah, some trust will be lost, and a few friendships end up obliterated, but those are the mild cases. Less mild: One phone call to the university and a minor (possibly not even factual) Incident could lead to expulsions, court cases, and severe legal trouble. Thankfully (or not?), this severity does not apply to the Nick and Ashley calamity. The problem stayed insulated for a while, and only a couple people found about what happened. The news did not spread far until the end of rush in January, right after winter break.

The rush process is judgmental, unnecessary, and objectively ridiculous, but *sometimes* frats face ethical or moral conflicts when deciding whether to give a bid. In Nick's case, ethics came into play heavily. Nick had been dropped from his top choice of frat because they found out about the Incident and did not want to deal with any scandal or legal trouble if they bid him. Nick's deletion from the first frat's process made it that much tougher for the frat that eventually gave him a bid to make their decision. Everyone basically agreed that Nick was a good kid. During rush, he was humble, charismatic, and respectful, so it was hard for many of the people at the final meeting to cut him for an Incident that "may or may not have occurred." As in most situations where rape is alleged, we mainly have the dramatically conflicting word of the two principal figures. *Someone* has to be lying (right?), and it is impossible to figure out the truth unless someone admits fault. In a college landscape, frat parties are commonly viewed as the primary location for sexual assault and date rape. Fraternities know this and aren't eager to add to the bad reputation. While it was common in the past to blame or ignore the woman who was raped, openly dismissing or minimizing Ashley's story in the current environment is not tenable.

So, what happened? Eventually, Nick received a bid and joined a frat. To this day, no one really knows the "truth" of what happened that night. Nick wasn't formally charged with assaulting Ashley, so the school didn't bring about any proceeding. Whether his fraternity was right to bid him, and whether Nick should be held responsible for what Ashley alleged, is up for debate. In an odd conundrum, the Incident was simultaneously earthshaking and had no impact whatsoever. Nick and Ashley were changed for life, I think, but absolutely nothing changed at school. Frat party hookups continue, alcohol is downed, telephone is played.

Wake up, repeat.

If my father was unable to harness the lessons of his painful childhood to become a better man, was I delusional for thinking I could?

Like Father, Like Son

Alex Parrish

The Baker stumbles into a clearing, distraught and alone. Moments ago, he abandoned his infant son to the arms of a strange princess. He had neither the courage nor the will to face the broken world after the death of his wife and, rather than take up the mantle of fatherly responsibility with strength and hope, he ran away. But before he goes where none can follow, The Baker's dead father, The Mysterious Man, appears quietly from behind a tree and muses that history is repeating itself; it turns out The Mysterious Man also abandoned The Baker as an infant out of guilt for incepting a magical curse upon his family, and he questions why his son is making the same mistake. In a duet titled "No More," they argue in haunting melody and disjointed rhyme, and reach a stark lyric together:

THE MYSTERIOUS MAN: We disappoint, we leave a mess
   We die but we don't . . .
THE BAKER: We disappoint in turn, I guess
   Forget though we won't . . .
BOTH: Like father, like son.

The dissonant strains resolve to a harmony as the song appears to be ending. Two damaged men have accepted an inevitability: no matter how often fathers disappoint or how long sons refuse to forget, sons will grow up to disappoint just the same.

I was eleven the first time I saw this scene from *Into the Woods*, a labyrinthine fairytale mashup musical by James Lapine and Stephen Sondheim. I was so captivated by "No More" that I scratched the DVD from watching it so many times. I needed this fictional father-son exploration to help me make sense of the very real, disastrous father-son relationship I faced when I left my room.

Any illusion that my father was a good man shattered the day he took my siblings and I aside to explain our mom to us. They fought so much because she was "crazy." She was emotionally unstable to the point of taking medication. She was so untrustworthy that anything she told us about him were lies. The blatancy of this scheme to turn us against our mother wiped the dirt from my windshield. As he talked, I thought about his aggressive physical intimidation, how he would demean us in public, and his endless gaslighting. This was a bad man.

I understand now that my father was a narcissistic manipulator who saw his children and wife of twenty-five years as opportunities to assert his dominance, but at that time, he was the Balrog to my Gandalf. I remember standing in front of my cowering sister and brother many times, facing down this monster of a parent far taller and stronger than me, and believing that if my shouts were loud enough, my logic sound enough, my arguments moral enough, a magical shield would appear: "YOU SHALL NOT PASS!"

My father finally left us when I was thirteen. The next five years were filled with brutal custody battles for my mother, but I began discarding his influence. For instance, I helped keep my siblings and I fed, in school, on time, and alive while my mother fought for our futures. I skimped on homework and researched psychology to help defend my siblings' in court affidavits. I opted out of a normal high school social life to preserve and rebuild a family that, it seemed, could have drowned in despair at any instant. I tried to prove that my father's selfishness, dominance, and arrogance had not been passed on to me.

At nineteen, in New York and pursuing an acting career, I was cast as The Baker in my acting studio's production of *Into the Woods*. I remember thinking, almost cynically, that I could use my "daddy issues" to drive my performance. But as I searched to understand why The Baker would abandon his child in "No More," I felt compelled to know why my real father had done what he'd done. I pestered my mother for answers.

She told me that my father had an antagonistic, abusive relationship with his father. My grandfather was so toxic, in fact, that my father cut off the relationship completely, as I had with my own father. The Mark Twain line, "History doesn't repeat itself, but it often rhymes," seemed dangerously true. If my father was unable to harness the lessons of his painful childhood to become a better man, was I delusional for thinking I could?

Back in rehearsal, performing The Baker became more challenging. For a chaotic scene in which The Baker and his Wife have a shouting match over who will take action, the stage director pressured me to dig into the darker aspects of the character, to embrace the masculinity of the anger, to demean and threaten and make The Baker's Wife listen to me, the way men often do. The clear line I'd always drawn between my characters and myself was suddenly blurry, my head filled with fathers and sons all vying for validation. I couldn't perform the scene; my body was forcibly preventing me from imitating the man I so feared to become.

Privately, though, I began to see that, despite all my efforts to never repeat my father's actions, I feel the same repulsive impulses he did. At times, my hand wants to become a fist, my sarcasm a demeaning insult, my insecurity a twisted manipulation. I feel my frustration edge into aggression, my sense of self-preservation transforming me into a selfish, angry monster. Worst of all, during those moments of darkness, the impulses don't feel wrong. It's enough to make any young man feel cursed.

I didn't revisit my long personal relationship with The Baker again until I saw *Now That We're Men*. The five boys at the center of the play trade barbs about sex, women, porn, danger, and fathers. Marcus, a charming ladies' man, describes how, when his mother got pregnant in her teens, his father ditched them. He grew up loving his mother and nursing self-righteous anger at his absent father. Then, he reveals that a girl he was dating missed a period and he, instead of rising to the occasion and succeeding where his father failed, ghosts her. Even though it turns out that the girl isn't pregnant, Marcus is tormented by shame. He agonizes over why his personal experience didn't shield him from committing his father's offense, why his quest to be a better man collapsed the moment he was called to step up.

Maybe Marcus, The Baker, The Mysterious Man, my grandfather, my father, and I are all damaged men destined to do damage. If having strong and loving mothers doesn't shield us, if suffering doesn't, if like-for-like experience doesn't teach us the right lessons, then what can possibly change this failure that passes from father to son, other than dying childless? Feeling very low, I dug out my scratched DVD of *Into the Woods* and searched Sondheim's songs for hope. And this time, I heard it.

The dissonant duet resolves into harmony with the line, "Like father, like son," which I had always read as meaning The Baker was fated to become his father. The Mysterious Man disappears into the mist, and The Baker is faced his inevitable failure. His emotion boils over as he sings:

How do you ignore all the witches, all the curses
   All the wolves, all the lies

The false hopes, the goodbyes, the reverses
All the wondering what even worse is still in
  store
All the children, all the giants . . .

But a stinging chord suddenly chokes his momentum. As the dissonance rings, he considers the joy that children bring and the destruction that giants bring. He considers the empty future waiting just beyond the trees and the burdened past beyond those at his back. He considers the hypocrisy, dark impulses, and false hopes of sons in the cycle of damage. Though The Mysterious Man may appear from the fog to strip away all pretense, The Baker himself can and must decide the difference between he and his father and all fathers that came before. We hear an open chord and: *"No more."*

The Baker takes a breath, turns around, and returns to both his son and the unknown awaiting him in the woods.

Contradictions and ironies come with the territory: for instance . . . becoming a man without ever having been a boy.

Man-ologues

Cooper Lee Bombardier

I *performed a version of this essay as an original monologue in* The Testosterone Testimonials: The Measure of a Man, *at the James A. Little Theater in Santa Fe in March 2008, alongside a rabbi in his eighties, a teenaged ex-gang member, the police chief, a state senator, and a reporter-turned-legislative analyst. The local newspaper,* The Santa Fe New Mexican, *listed me alongside the others as "transsexual Cooper Lee Bombardier" in its pre-performance coverage. Needless to say, this was deeply irritating. The other performers were named by their professions; I was reduced a piece of my medical history. The fact that I was an artist, a writer, ran a statewide program for at-risk youth, or was the host of a monthly cabaret was made invisible by my transness. This is the plight of the token.*

The Testosterone Testimonials *was, unsurprisingly, modeled somewhat after* The Vagina Monologues. *I jokingly referred to my contributions as my Mangina Man-ologue. The point was to trouble the notion of manhood and provide a view into a multivalent and (hopefully) non-toxic masculinity. I performed to a packed theater filled with cisgender, non-queer people; because of this, the monologue veers toward the didactic. In 2008, I felt I needed to convince others to accept my humanity.*

Like all of the other men here tonight, I knew that I would one day grow up to be a man. Unlike the other men here, perhaps, on the day I was born, the delivering doctor proclaimed me a baby girl.

By telling you that I am a transgender man, you may already be thinking that my life is far more exciting and exotic than it really is. Perhaps you have visions of *The Oprah Winfrey Show* or chair-throwing "trannies" on *Jerry Springer*. Even worse, maybe images from *Boys Don't Cry* or *The Silence of the Lambs*.

My life is not particularly exotic, but it certainly has had its twists and turns. I lived in this world for more than thirty years as female, at least outwardly. While I never felt completely comfortable as female, or identifying as female, I do feel grateful for the knowledge I have gleaned from those experiences. Sometimes I feel deep sorrow that I was not born male. Sometimes I regret that I did not transition to male much earlier in my life. Still, I know that I would not be the man I am today if I hadn't been the woman I became in my twenties.

I struggled with my gender identity from within the thriving dyke punk art scene that ruled San Francisco in the 1990s. This was an incredible community filled with self-loving, creative queers. In 1996, I finally shared my questioning of my gender with this warm sisterhood. The reaction was overwhelmingly negative. The message was that, in the queer community, I was valuable—celebrated—as a masculine woman. But if I pushed a bit further into my deepest sense of who I was and became a man, then I was a traitor and a sell-out.

I didn't want to cross to the dark side, rife with male privilege. I couldn't abide the thought of disappearing into the ether of straight, white male-dom. But this view was just from within my small, albeit fabulous, queer world. How would I be received *outside* of that enclave, in the hypermasculine worlds of construction and welding and carpentry where I worked, for instance? Or by my family? How would the rest of the straight world see me? Would my maleness be validated or belittled and picked apart? Would my life feel peaceful and whole, or would I be harassed and subjected to violence even beyond what I had thus far experienced?

Adding to those virtuous concerns was something a bit more ego-driven: I feared losing my "outlaw status" as a strong, wild, and free-loving butch dyke! As a butch woman, I simply did not blend in. I was *seen*, and I was used to being recognized for what I was— well, *almost* what I was. I liked the fact that straight guys treated me as a buddy/dude/confidante/flirtation. It's hard to explain the dynamic, but if you're a masculine woman or a guy who hangs with same, you know what I mean. As a butch dyke, I was sexy and vital. As a man, the unspoken message seemed to be that I would be shallow, boring, typical, and unnecessary.

And then, of course, there was my own trauma. My youth was spent painfully aware of how differently my brothers were treated. For years, I had longed for amends to be made to me by my father, who was often abusive. As a "woman" working in the trades of construction and welding, I worked twice as hard, but it seemed I was still seen as half as good as less-qualified men in the shop. The truth was that I totally got the analysis of male privilege and power that my dyke comrades and friends lobbed at me—and I agreed. I understood that "playing" with gender was one thing (though to me it never felt like play; it was just my *gender*), but becoming a man was another thing entirely. I was terrified that I might lose the only community that ever felt like home to me, but I also felt terrified to not live my life in the best way I could see fit.

In order to make this transition, I had to repair my relationships with men in my life and repair my relationship with the idea of men in general. I had to accept the fact that, even if I didn't want to "have to choose" a gender, I would rather live this life in a male body.

Even after that realization, I lived for many years as trans in name and pronoun—and in my internal sense of self—only. My girlfriend, friends, and brother knew that I preferred male pronouns and felt male, but I was reluctant to avail myself of the medical options available to me as a transgender person. I am the kind of person who must be begged to take Theraflu when I am sick, so the idea of being on a powerful medication for the rest of my life was overwhelming. I worried about creating health problems in an otherwise healthy body. Even if I had the money for surgery, which I didn't, I was terrified of being put under general anesthesia. I struggled with whether transition was the right for me. One trans guy told me he had never felt so "at home" in his own body; another told me, "You can choose to become a man, but you can't choose the man you'll become." Another man likened transition to diving into a deep lake and having no idea where you would come back up. These ideas filled me with dread that I would have little control over how I would change. I had to make peace with the fact that I could not simply pick and choose how I would be changed by being a man in the world. And I had to face facts: the changes I longed to experience were not going to happen by themselves.

I started T—testosterone—in 2002. The conventional wisdom is that testosterone makes a raging, aggressive, and irritable person out of you. It blunts healthy emotions, like crying and empathy. Yet I have felt calmer than I ever thought would be possible since I started on T. I can still easily access my empathy and sensitive emotions. The difference is that, before, I felt like an all-feeling, uber-sensitive sea-anemone floating through life and picking up everyone else's emotions; now I feel like I have a little more of a choice in what feelings I absorb. I still cry at sappy moments in movies or when someone I really love is hurting; I don't cry over, say, cat food commercials. I am less attached to the extreme people-pleasing behaviors that I was imbued with as a female-born person. I am quite happy to help out and try to take care of those around me, but I don't do so at the expense of my own peace or sanity. I am okay setting boundaries and saying what I need and what I mean.

Being on T and being a transgender person requires an enormous sense of humor. In fact, not taking myself too seriously has been integral to my survival. Contradictions and ironies come with the territory— for instance, experiencing puberty and male-pattern balding at the same time. Or getting a birthday card from my mother with my chosen name in quotation marks. Yearning for handsome sideburns but growing a neckbeard first. Getting quizzical looks from people when I mention my high school boyfriend. Or becoming a man without ever having been a boy.

After my first shot of testosterone, I dreamt that I would wake up the next day covered in hair like a teenage werewolf, horny and uncouth, muscles bulging, running around like a wild animal. Instead, I felt a sense of belonging in my own body that I have never before known. I had no idea how much space anxiety around my gender took up until it wasn't there anymore. I have so much more energy to give to my loved ones now. And I have much more room to be compassionate for other folks, too, since I have learned to give that to myself.

Your weakness is pitiful, the tears that roll down your face is just a sign of disgrace.

MisUnderstood

Caleb Grandoit

What do you want from me?
Your weakness is pitiful, the tears that roll
down your face is just a sign of disgrace
What do you want from me?
Stand up tall, shoulder length apart and when you
respond to me . . .
It's yes sir, anything less won't get you far
What do you want from me?
Get more girls that's a given
The more sex you have your spot will forever be
solidify
What do you want from me?
Your pockets to stay full, can't be broke you'll be
mistaken for a fool
What do you want from me?
Be a man
*But the pain I see, I can't help but wear it on my
sleeve*
Be a man
Girls just aren't attracted to me
Be a man
Numbers don't determine me fulfilling my purpose
Be a man
My dick doesn't always need to be itched
Be a man

See here lays the glitch between you and me
Be a man
You keep telling what to be, not realizing the truth I see
Be a man
This made up illusion, pretending as if it's a constitution
Be a man
See I think you're scared to be who you really are
Be a man
Because no one ever told you that just being you is a beautiful art
Be a man
Why can't you shut up and just listen to me
Be a man
It is a shame because you keep repeating the same history
Be a man
His story was his. Stop living his and just live
Be a man
Trying to live up to a standard, never having a chance to be a kid
Be a man
Sometimes I feel like laying in a ditch, where my existence wouldn't even be missed
Be a MAN!

Men are longing to be gentle, longing to be able to cry, longing to be able to be lost, longing not to be so alone, longing not to have to carry this insane burden of perfection and adoration.

In Recovery with Eve Ensler: A Conversation

Jennifer Baumgardner and Jordan Eliot

If you are looking to combine theater with activism, then Eve Ensler might just be your guru. A successful playwright since the 1980s, her career exploded with her 1996 dramatic juggernaut, *The Vagina Monologues*. It was a long-running hit off Broadway but, crucially, a staple on college campuses and in local communities, with thousands of local productions performed each year. Eve made the play accessible by waiving licensing fees as long as it is performed in February and the performance is used to raise funds and awareness about violence against all women and girls (cisgender, transgender, and those who hold fluid identities that are subject to gender-based violence). Since founding the V-Day movement, Eve has written many more plays and books—including *I Am an Emotional Creature*, *The Good Body*, and *In the Body of the World*—and founded the campaign One Billion Rising, as well as cofounded (with Christine Schuler Deschryver and 2018 Nobel Peace Prize Laureate Dr. Denis Mukwege) City of Joy, a sanctuary and revolutionary center in Bukavu, Democratic Republic of the Congo for women survivors of sexual terrorism.

On a cold April day in 2019, Eve sat down with

Jordan Eliot, who originated the role of Andrew in *Now That We're Men*, and Jennifer Baumgardner, to talk about the kinds of visionary change we want for men *and* women, and how feminism and theater can provide it.

JENNIFER: You are a transformative activist who has shifted culture around sexual violence and female agency for decades. Your primary vehicle has been theater. Can you talk about why theater is a powerful tool?

EVE: Theater is one of the most radical and transformational art forms. It happens in the dark, with strangers in the present, in the flesh. You, as audience, co-create the play with the actors. Each show is different, surprising, dangerous, depending on the energy and the crowd. This can be catalytic. The theater has the potential to be an embodied experience, to literally change one right there in the room. I have seen people walk out of *The Vagina Monologues* changed; a penny dropped. Perspective altered, body reclaimed.

JENNIFER: You've been in the vagina space for a long time—there have been tens of thousands of college and community productions of *The Vagina Monologues* over the past two decades. I know women are transformed by performing it and seeing it, but what do you hear from men about their experience with the play?

EVE: Well, I used to joke that *The Vagina Monologues* is loved by all women who see it and hated by men who don't. Initially, men didn't come unless they were dragged by wives, girlfriends, sisters, or friends. That has changed greatly over the years. Now it's half-and-half in the audiences, and, this past year, a good chunk of the many hundreds of V-Day productions were directed by men. What I hear from men about the play is that they learn so much. They have been afraid to ask questions about sex and pleasure. They date women who have been abused, and they want to be more supportive and don't know how. They become more aware of what women experience and feel, and I believe this makes them more sensitive.

JENNIFER: Men are socialized to be ignorant and repressed around women's bodily experiences. It reminds me of this artist, Vinnie Angel, who asked a childhood friend casually what the worst thing was that had ever happened to her (they were doing a magazine quiz). She told him that she'd been gang-raped in high school. He was shocked by her answer, but also shaken by the fact that he hadn't known, hadn't supported her. He began picking at the origins of this silence/willful ignorance and came to see that there is an unstated social pact: Everything connected to vaginas is secret. For him, it began with periods, when he felt like

he had to pretend he didn't see tampons in his friend's purse or whatever. That silence leads to silence around sexual violence, he felt. He distributed thousands of tampon cases emblazoned with his name so that he could model interacting openly with a female "secret."

EVE: Ignorance is big. A big problem we have in this country is the lack of real sex education—helping boys and girls know what they desire, *learn* what feels good, what healthy sex and pleasure feels like and looks like. We're so afraid to talk about sex. So many people just kind of fumble in the dark, without satisfying their partners or teaching their partners what they desire. The silence around sex allows for all kinds of terrible things to happen. We need to see sex as something beautiful, necessary, life-affirming, as opposed to something ugly and sinful. Satisfying, loving sex would actually eradicate violence. So often boys are aggressive because they feel like they should know what they are doing, and they don't. Rather than learning, they perform, and often that performance mirrors the worst in men.

JENNIFER: Porn plays an enormous role in *Now That We're Men*. It's so common that it's almost not controversial, but it's also warping the characters who watch it; they are seeing confusing or debasing images that don't relate to their feelings about the girls they like. My son is fourteen years old, and I have talked to him about watching porn. He once mentioned that he doesn't know any other way to learn how to have sex. I said, *Oh my God, I didn't realize that's why you were watching it. I thought it was for masturbation, not education.*

EVE: Until we can teach what appropriate, healthy, loving, mutual, consenting sex is, boys and girls will learn about it from pornography. If you look at the way a lot of young women think they have to behave, it's based on pornography. It's all performative, objectifying and often disembodied. It's not intimate, it's not involved, it's not looking at one another, it's not connecting, it's not letting sex grow out of your mutual experience and be what you particularly want it to be.

JENNIFER: How did you learn how to have sex that is healthy?

EVE: Feminism and masturbation. Sex workshops teaching you about your body and how to have an orgasm, reading people who were talking about what sexuality is. Talking to other women who had more experience.

Masturbation is critical for everyone. It's practice, it teaches you what you like and don't like, what brings you to orgasm. Then you are able to teach your partner. If you don't know what gives you pleasure, how can you show someone else?

JENNIFER: It's deeper than women not knowing

what they like: It's being so inhibited that they can't articulate any directions, even in their own minds.

EVE: Most women don't take the time to explore because they don't believe they have a right to pleasure. They don't allow themselves the time it takes to give themselves pleasure. I've talked to many women who say they don't masturbate, which is like saying, "I don't read." If you touch yourself, feel yourself, and get who you are, you are literate.

The second piece is feeling comfortable and confident and unashamed enough to say, "Excuse me, that's not where it feels good; it feels good over there," or, "When you do that, it doesn't do it for me, but if you go slower, if you inch up, if you take your time."

JENNIFER: **What messages should we be sending to young children, pre-puberty?**

EVE: Stop making sex "bad." Sex is the manifestation of your life force, love, and intimacy. What you feel about sex, you directly or indirectly communicate to your child—you don't even have to speak it; body language communicates things.

I would give my child books to read about good sex, with pictures. The earlier the better. If you know what sex is—you know what your rights are, you learn what consent is, you know what your desires are, you know what speed you need to go— there is a better chance you'll be calling the shots.

If you're in the dark, then you can be easily over-whelmed and taken in directions you don't want to be taken in.

JENNIFER: How did you get the idea to write the apology you had never gotten from your father?

EVE: I was thinking about how many times I have heard women tell their stories in twenty-one years; how many silences I've heard broken; how many people have spoken out; how many Take Back the Night marches, pro-choice marches, risings and V-days I've attended. I was thinking of all of this, and then I thought: How many men have actually authentically, deeply, publicly apologized for sexual abuse? Have I *ever* heard a man ever publicly apologize for sexual abuse in 16,000 years of patriarchy? The answer was no.

I started to think this must be pretty central to everything. We're calling out men, we're speaking these truths, telling our stories, but it feels as if we are at a stalemate. Where are the men willing to do deep self-interrogation, look at their histories, look at what brought them there, investigate the *why* of what they've done and the details of what they've done, and get to know themselves in order to trans-form themselves into other kinds of men incapable of being violent again?

It occurred to me that I've been waiting for an apology from my father for sixty years. He's been dead for half of that time. I thought, *I'm going to write the words I need to hear in his voice. I am going to go inside him and let him speak the words that will finally free me.*

JENNIFER: What happened when you began "channeling" him?

EVE: Well, it was a conjuring. He told me things about him I've never known before. I began to understand his trajectory. I saw what in his childhood laid the groundwork for him to become a sadist and a sexual abuser. I saw what in the culture of patriarchy and toxic masculinity had damaged him.

JENNIFER: In *The Apology*, your father recounts a time when your cat was hit by a car. Your dad cradled the cat and allowed his broken parts to come out. It reminded me that some of the most stern or patriarchal men that I've known have had this mysterious soft side for little kids and animals.

EVE: It's a place where men are allowed to express tenderness. One of the reasons why there is so much incest and sexual abuse and violence is because men *aren't* allowed to express or feel tenderness. Love embraces all. In my father's case, he was adored, but adoration is not love; it is a projection of someone's idealized image onto you, which you are then forced to live up to. Love embraces all of you: your vulnerability, your tenderness, your tears, your sorrow, your doubts. My father had to banish all those feelings and push them underground. They eventually metastasized into another persona, which he called Shadow Man. And that disassociate self, as catalyzed at my birth, as he flooded with feelings of tenderness, took his capacity to hold or process, since no one had allowed these feelings in or towards him. He couldn't allow himself to just be open to that tenderness. He had to do something to it. Crush it. Hurt it. Rape it. Dominate it. Make it go away. Patriarchy is an equal destroyer. It robs men of their hearts and humanity. We need to bring up boys so differently. We need to let them feel and cry and express wonder and doubt and curiosity. We need to stop robbing them of their humanity.

JENNIFER: Jordan, your piece in this book deals with crying as a boy.

JORDAN: In my family, crying was always allowed at home. I had to adjust myself to the expectations of school; it wasn't acceptable to cry as a boy. If I was scared of the movie we were watching at lunch, I'd get, *Why should you be scared?* I so wanted the self I had to be at school to be my whole self, but then I also had a home that fostered my real self, and I had to put that part away in the real world.

EVE: When you grow up in a radical or transformative house, how do you then function in society? It makes me think of mothers at the playground, when someone smacks their boy, and they don't want him to hit back—but then they think, *Am I preparing him to live in this world?* At some point, though, we've all got to be willing to prepare our children not for the current world, but to be agents of change.

JORDAN: Crying is banned for young boys. As you get older, the painful issue is being forced into bro culture. You are banned from participating in anything that makes you seem feminine, God forbid.

EVE: Everyone—men, women, boys, girls—is trained *not* to be a girl. That makes me think it must be *very* powerful to be a girl, if everyone's being told not to be one.

JENNIFER: How does male entitlement work? In *The Apology*, it seems to come out of this tremendous emptiness.

EVE: A lot of boys are adored, which *sounds* good, but is actually distorting and dehumanizing. *You are the boy; you are the crown of the crowns. You're going to fulfill the family's dreams; you're going to move everything forward, divine right of kings.*

Again, adoration isn't love. If you're the "perfect" son and do something wrong, you fall from that pedestal. It puts men into this very precarious position where they have to build up this fake identity, which isn't grounded in being able to fail, discover, get lost, be in mystery, or have tenderness and vulnerability. I think boys get really enraged by that, like, *Why can't I be a human being?* On one hand, you're getting total privilege and power, but on the other hand, your humanity is erased.

You pass on privilege by getting boys to believe

that they are the best, on top, in charge, perfect, worthy of glorification, and that's how you keep this continuum alive. In fact, I think what most boys know, particularly in young ages, is that it's just not true. So, they feel fraudulent—*Why am I being told I'm perfect when I'm a mess? I don't know stuff, and I want to cry all the time. I have total doubts, but I'm not allowed to express my doubts and needs.* I think our boys end up fulfilling a patriarchal fantasy of their parents, rather than letting themselves be these beautiful, tender, evolving, messy creatures. So, then they don't have to do the work, asking themselves real questions—*Who am I? How do I behave? How should I treat people?*—because they own the world.

I wrote *The Apology* to be a blueprint for men to see what an apology might look like. This is how they could go about actually beginning to repair and reckon and account for bad behavior that has been really harmful for women.

What's going to compel the privileged to change themselves when they have all the power and privilege? What my father really taught me in this book is that men are in prisons, men are in hell, men are not happy, men are alone, men are isolated even when they are around people. Men are longing to be gentle, longing to be able to cry, longing to be able to be lost, longing not to be so alone, longing not to have to carry this insane burden of perfection and adoration. How do we help men understand that that is the outcome of patriarchy?

JENNIFER: It seems that people with a lot of privilege or entitlement have almost no capacity to deal with scary feelings like guilt and shame. Your father obviously knew that he molested you and that he treated you cruelly, undermined you, and said you made things up. These can't be things he was proud of. Would it have annihilated your father or his self-image to apologize?

EVE: My father says in the book, "To be an apologist is to be a traitor." I think that's how men feel. Once a man admits he was wrong and he knew he was wrong, the whole story of patriarchy comes tumbling down. What we need is a cadre of brave men to come forward to be the brave gender traitors. Men, start making the sincere, deep, rigorous, humble, vulnerable apologies, because when that starts to happen, I believe patriarchy will start to fall. It's clearly a central column keeping it in place.

JENNIFER: I want that new world, too! As we are making that new reality, do you have advice for young people for staying sane, healthy, and present, given the current threats to their bodies and the miseducation they receive?

EVE: Sure. I'd say that these actions could be useful:

— Create a counter narrative of seeing and protecting one another.

— Imagination is our most powerful tool. Envision where we are going.

—In the face of crassness and dissociation, be *more* sensitive, connected and *more* in tune. Assume everyone is traumatized, work from there.

—Make sure everyone's included, leave no one on the margins. If you have privilege, share it.

—Have meaningful sex, by which I mean sensual, beautiful, kind, loving touch and connection that is deepening. Marvin Gaye said it: sexual healing is healing.

—Dance. All the time.

There are countless spaces
where boys can perform masculinity,
but there are almost no places
where boys are free to be whole
human beings.

Scenes from the Making of
Now That We're Men

Katie Cappiello

2015: FIRST MEETING

It is early on a fall Sunday. I sit by myself in a tiny rehearsal studio in downtown Manhattan, nervously sipping a coffee, wrestling with whether my new project is a terrible idea.

"Do you think they're actually going to open up to *me?*" I'd asked my boyfriend before I rushed out of our Brooklyn apartment that morning. "I mean, I'm a thirty-five-year-old woman."

"Uh, maybe not, to be honest," he'd said. "But you're going to find out today, right?"

Right. So here I am, waiting for a group of high school boys to join me for an experimental workshop.

I wanted to hear about their lives, their thoughts on coming of age, and their feelings about sex and gender. Over nine years as a feminist playwright and director, I'd explored the challenges facing girls and young women. My plays portrayed social media madness, first-person stories of girls who'd been trafficked into sex work, and real-life accounts of people who'd undergone female genital mutilation. One of my plays, *SLUT* (which debuted in 2013), toured widely and presented opportunities to engage in honest conversations about sex and sexual assault with people of all genders across the United States, from Fargo to

Los Angeles. In intimate workshops and talk-backs, I was struck by how desperately men and boys needed a space to talk about sex, masculinity, and their fears. It became clearer to me that boys, too, are warped by rape culture and are just as confused about consent as girls are. The boys I met were struggling to live up to impossible standards of masculinity, just as they were dealing with the tumult of growing up and exploring their sexual selves.

If we want to effectively address issues like slut-shaming, revenge porn, trolling, sexual harassment, sexual assault, homophobia, violence, binge drinking, group aggression—to name a few common, pernicious issues—we have to care about what it means to be young and male today. The *SLUT* tour left me with an urgent sense that I needed to develop *something* with boys. But *what?*

At the studio, I remove a stack of blank printer paper and some pens from my backpack, and shoot another look at the clock: 10:58 a.m. I make a quick note in my journal: *Your job is to LISTEN. Let them know they can trust you. This isn't about judgment or evaluation. It's an open exchange of ideas.*

Jordan arrives first, perfectly on time—something that would become a trend over the next three years. Jordan is tall with a perpetually warm smile; he's a self-proclaimed "sensitive person" and a straight-A student who moonlights as a professional dog walker. I first met Jordan when he was an eight-year-old puppet master—literally. He brought elaborate puppets to acting class and incorporated them into his scenes.

Now sixteen, he plants himself on the floor right next to me like an old friend and we chat about our latest Netflix binge (as we do), until—

Fred bursts into the room, raking his hands through his bed-head hair, his blue eyes energized. Fifteen and a sophomore, he drops his backpack onto the floor, claps Jordan on the shoulder, gives me a hug hello, and launches into an animated story about his delayed train ride from the Upper West Side. Fred is a movie buff, a prolific writer, an always-on-the-go school newspaper editor, and a card-carrying feminist—by which I mean, he reads Rebecca Solnit and he wants to talk to you about it. I met Fred when he was in seventh grade; he'd asked if he could contribute a piece to a book I was putting together about rape culture. I said sure, and Fred delivered a 1500-word essay on the impact of pornography on his life. He was twelve at the time.

Alphonso and Rayshawn are next, both carrying bags from McDonald's—Alphonso, sixteen, with his headphones still on; Rayshawn, fourteen, strapped with a SpongeBob backpack "ironically." There are daps and introductions all around, and the boys engage in a little get-to-know-you talk. Alphonso makes the trip from Newark, New Jersey. He's quick to laugh and crack a joke, he's a drummer and a rapper, and he's also a deacon's son and an active member of his parish. In his first year in my acting class, when he was in eighth grade, he told me with a beaming smile that he had to leave early because he had something important to celebrate: His town was putting his picture on a billboard for being Student of the Month.

Rayshawn, who at 6'3" towers over everyone, is still the little brother of the group—the youngest, the wildest. He's a member of his high school basketball team in Queens, and a proud big brother and babysitter to his three-year-old sister (she *dominates* his Instagram). The first day I met Rayshawn, I asked him if he'd done anything exciting over the weekend, he said, "Yeah, man. Me and my friends, we surfed the subway—"

"What?" I said. I'd never heard of this.

He answered nonchalantly, "Like, we hung onto the back of the subway, you know? Fucking crazy. Scary as hell. Probably a little bit dumb."

Rayshawn and Alphonso make themselves comfortable, all sprawled out, resting their heads on their bags and digging into their French fries. I make a note in my journal: *Free with their bodies right off the bat. Not afraid to take up space.*

Fred's eyes bulge when he sees the food, and then, without even the slightest hesitation: "Hey, man, can I get a fry?" Rayshawn shrugs and offers Fred the bag. Fred digs in and boldly tales a handful of fries.

Rayshawn, kind of stunned, doesn't hold back. "Yo, Fred, yo—I don't even know you, bro, and you're taking all my fucking fries?!"

"No, man, it's just a few!" Fred lies. We erupt in laughter and I make note of it all: *Fearless. No formality. Settling into roles already. RELAXED.*

And I feel myself begin to relax, like I usually do once kids are in the room. I allow myself a hopeful thought. *Maybe this would actually work.*

Caleb, seventeen, entered the space with quiet confidence and calmness. We met in acting class. When I asked him if he was interested in participating in the project, he said, "Yes," before I could even finish my sentence. But when I told him we'd be meeting on Sundays, his face fell. "Would it be okay if I'm a little late? I go to church with my mom on Sundays. I can make sure we go to earlier services so I can be here, but I really don't like to miss church."

Caleb could easily be a contestant on *World of Dance*. He's a poet, a budding filmmaker. He's stopped by the NYPD on the regular. And he's been the leader of this cast since that very first day.

Our group had assembled. The cold, closet-like room warms up quickly, their chatter and big laughs bouncing off the walls. I grab my paper and give them each a little stack and a pen. They look at me expectantly. It is time to find out if they would open up to me.

"Thanks so much for being here, you guys," I start. "Um, I'm not exactly sure what I want the end product to be at this point, but I want to start off by saying I'm excited to spend this time with you. I've known each of you for a long time and I respect you greatly. We're in this room together because I trust you and you trust me. So, I need you to know this: Nothing you tell me will make me appreciate you any less, okay? The only way this will work is if we're honest with each other. I'm open to hearing all you have to say, okay? Sound good?"

They nod. Suddenly, it is first-day-of-school quiet.

Until, Rayshawn: "Cool, cool. Let's get to it, then." Then he takes off his hoodie and resumes munching on his food. He is wearing a Stüssy T-shirt, and it takes me a minute for the shirt's design to register: a photo of a sprawled-out, naked woman with a black censor bar across her face.

I add to my notes: *T-SHIRT W/ THE NUDE = WHY WE'RE HERE.* And I say, "Okay! Great!"

Kickstarting an honest conversation about sex and gender politics with a group of high school boys is not the easiest thing. It's not something they often (or ever) do—not in a moderated setting, and not even with friends. While "safe spaces" for girls are exploding in numbers (I've created some of those spaces in theaters and schools across the country), it continues to be rare for young men to be offered a similar opportunity.

I often hear some version of, "*All* spaces are safe spaces for men and boys." This is simply not true. There are countless spaces where boys can perform masculinity, but there are almost no places where boys are free to be whole human beings.

This is uncharted territory for the guys and me. Before we even attempt to dig deep, I give Jordan, Fred, Alphonso, Rayshawn, and Caleb three writing prompts. I don't specify what I'm looking for (I don't know what I am looking for). I ask them to write anything that comes to mind, stream-of-consciousness-style.

"It's nothing I will see," I assure them. "It's just a process for organizing your thoughts." They jot down these prompts:

1. Dude, you're a fag.
2. Guys want to have sex all the time.
3. My friend did the craziest fucking thing . . .

They go to work. An hour later, everyone is sharing:

"I had this best friend when I was a kid. And he was a little quiet and he would never look at the porn links me and my other friends were passing around. I mean, we were only in, like, third grade, but we were looking at this shit. So, this one time, I forced him to watch. I held him down so he had to see it. I told him he was a fag if he didn't watch . . . I think about that day all the time."

"Some people just don't believe I've never had sex. Like they think just 'cause I'm male that I'm, like, trying to have sex all the time, or that I have no sense of self control or whatever. When you're a guy, if you don't want to have sex 'cause you're not ready or you're just not interested right then, everyone thinks it's 'cause something's wrong with you—like you must have a small dick or you must be gay or a pussy or whatever."

"Guys are up on girls all the time at my school. Grabbing asses and tits in the hallway. In front of everyone. No one says anything. I don't say anything. 'Cause, like, what am I gonna say, honestly? And it's not like people don't get suspended or get in trouble at

my school for all kinds of shit, they do! But never for that. It's like it happens and no one cares."

"My friends pass around the nudes girls send them. I've done it too. The girl didn't know, so it's not like she was really impacted in any real way . . . Also, I heard somewhere it's illegal to text nudes and whatever. Is that actually illegal? How?"

"I was a big crier when I was a kid. If I got nervous or if people were mean to me or something like that, I would tear up. And I remember kids being really judgmental about it—teachers, too. I don't think I'm allowed to be as emotional, I guess, as I really am. Not emotional in a dramatic way, but just in a human way—there's not a lot of situations for me to express my feelings."

Lots of nodding heads and *I hear that* or *Yeah, same for me.* They begin to sync up with one another, and once the floodgates open, it's a challenge to wrap things up. Over the coming weeks, we ponder things like:

Who is harmed when the words "pussy," "gay," and "fag" are thrown around in the halls of middle and high school?

What does it feel like to participate in a culture where some of the most popular video games on the market give points when players (mostly young and male) rape and kill women?

What does it mean when, on average, a boy first sees hardcore porn between eight and eleven years old, or when some of the biggest names in music tell *Rolling Stone* the best thing they've ever done in their lives is pimp women?

What do boys think when professional athletes beat their girlfriends and wives, and then not only have women lining up to date them, but have promotional contracts with some of the biggest brands out there?

What do boys think, feel, and learn when female classmates are called out for dress code violations, implying that the bare midriffs, knees, and shoulders of girls are offensive, distracting, inappropriate—or slutty?

What dynamics do individual boys observe at home with their parents and siblings?

Sharing stories fuels the dialogue. Storytelling will be the way I invite others to join us. After six weeks of working together for twelve hours a week, I've written the play *Now That We're Men*.

2015: SHOWTIME

The evening before our first performance, I hold an intimate, open dress rehearsal in the same small studio in downtown Manhattan. No one has seen a glimpse of the play or even read a scene, but a sold-out crowd is coming our way in less than twenty-four hours. The boys and I are on edge: *Is the play strong enough? Does it make sense? Is it offensive? Too much? Entertaining? Would the intention be clear? Would people walk away with* something?

My friends Charlotte, who's in her twenties, and

Cathryn, who's in her fifties, sit on plastic folding chairs as the cast moves like puppies from scene to scene—dancing, humping benches, wrestling each other over Chinese food, tearing up, directly engaging the audience during their monologues—all while exploring topics like depression, deep-throating, penis size, parental expectations, fetishes, and friendship.

After the play's final moment, I run to Charlotte and Cathryn, who are sitting quietly.

"So," I say, "what do you think?"

"It's startling," Cathryn says. "I don't quite have the words yet."

YIKES.

Then she turns and asks the boys directly, "Are you worried about putting all of this out there? Are you comfortable saying all of this?"

The boys look at each other, clearly nervous and conflicted. Then Alphonso says, "Yeah, I'm worried. And no, I'm not totally comfortable—because these are uncomfortable subjects—but I'm glad I'm one of the guys saying it out loud."

Then Charlotte: "Have you ever participated in something like this before? These types of discussions?"

They all shake their heads.

"I actually don't think this conversation is happening anywhere but in here," Jordan says. "But we've all been changed by this experience. I think the audience will be changed, too."

Cathryn, with the hint of a smile, offers, "It's fucking brave."

The next night is our first real performance. The

theater at New York City's The New School is buzzing. All the boys' families are sitting close to the front.

I stand in the back so I can pace—and watch both the boys and the audience. People laugh, gasp, and even groan with discomfort, and they're on their feet when the cast takes a final bow. I do talk-backs after almost every play I write, but this one lasts longer than others, almost ninety minutes. No one wants to leave. There are many questions.

Do boys really talk like that?

How do we make this better?

What can we do about porn?

Who is responsible for this culture?

What's next?

What's next?

What's next?

And, even, *Why would you go from creating feminist theater to writing a play about boys?*

"This is feminist theater," I say simply.

Alphonso scoffs. I look at him and we share a laugh. Then, he looks right at his dad and says, "No, it's not. Not to me. It's just good theater."

I counter, "It's feminist theater to me. Feminism is about being whole. It's a movement that advocates for every person's right to be a complete, complex person. And right now, boys are not given the emotional space to fully be who they are. One of feminism's goals is to deconstruct the ills of the patriarchy for *everyone*, including boys and men. I believe this play does that."

Alphonso shrugs like, *There goes Katie, on her soapbox.*

"And, as for what's next," I continue, "does anyone have any ideas?"

"Get it up and running as soon as possible," someone shouts.

"Bring it to schools," adds another.

So, I do both for the next year and a half.

2016: NEW YORK

I start touring with back-to-back performances of *Now That We're Men and SLUT,* harking back to the double-header movie features of my childhood. I worry if it will attract audiences. Almost three hours of theater is a commitment, like *Hamlet* or the opera.

But we pack the house *every* time.

Observing audience reactions to both plays is wild and instructive. They laugh, complete with knee-slapping and keeling over, through the boys' antics, then stare in horror and judgment at the girls' frank, playful talk of sexuality. There is disbelief and shock in the final moments of *Now That We're Men* as audiences realize one of these lovable guys just raped his girlfriend. Seeing the boys' play first gives way to a more nuanced understanding of the sexual assault in *SLUT.*

During one of the talk-backs at Dixon Place on New York's Lower East Side, a man in his fifties says he is "disturbed by how hyper-sexed and raunchy" the characters are in *SLUT.* He wonders why they say "'fuck' so many times" and he questions the "strength" of their—and my—vocabulary.

A young woman in the audience asks if he is put off

by the boys' vulgar language in *Now That We're Men*. He responds, "No, because that's how boys realistically behave." The audience erupts in agreement and disagreement. The cast and audience debate gender expectations and stereotypes for the rest of the post-show discussion.

Why is it entertaining when boys are offensive and pushing boundaries, but cringeworthy when girls do the same thing?

Why are we so empathetic to boys in trouble and less so to the girls who call them out?

Why do boys feel they need to posture all the time when it comes to sex—or anything?

But don't girls do the same thing?

Maybe this is why we need to keep working to dismantle the gender binary, am I right?! (Snaps all around.)

2016: BROOKLYN

The play has a run at the Maroney Theater, part of St. Francis College. On the opening night, an entire high school basketball team shows up an hour and a half early, before the box office opens, and wanders in while we finish last-minute lighting changes. We stare at them as they make their way to a cluster of seats, carrying pizza boxes and fountain sodas.

Me: "Hey, guys—"

Basketball Kid 1: "What's up? We're here for the show."

Me: "Great. It doesn't start for a while and we're still rehearsing."

Basketball Kid 2: "Oh shit. Our bad!" They laugh and tease each other, mumbling among themselves.

And then, Basketball Kid 3: "Um, Miss, could we just stay and watch and eat our food? We've never seen a rehearsal before, so . . ."

Me: "Absolutely. Have you ever been to a play before?"

Basketball Kid 4: "No."

Me: "How'd you hear about this one?"

Basketball Kid 4: "Someone from our school was like, *You should go, it's free*, and we go to school near here."

Me: "Nice. Well . . . welcome."

These kids sit on the edge of their seats the entire show, blissfully ignorant of traditional (stodgy) "theater etiquette."

Rayshawn is a minute into his monologue about his character Derrick's first time having sex. *And we do it and it's kind of great. 'Cause I'm having fucking sex, okay?! But, um, it was over in like . . .* and one of the basketball kids shoots up his hand like he's in class and yells, "Three seconds?!"

Rayshawn bursts into laughter, walks up to the kid (who was flashing the biggest smile in the audience), and responds, "Nah, like nine seconds! But clearly you feel me, bro!"

The audience starts clapping and *Ohhhhhh*-ing.

Basketball kid responds with glee, "Yo, I fucking been there, son! I'm telling you—I know! Don't feel bad, bro!"

I am thrilled. This live theater is really *alive*.

Near the end of the performance, a cell phone goes off—always a bummer during a play—and one of the basketball kids answers it urgently, "Imma have to call you back. I'm at a play and they're talking about deep-throating and this one kid did something fucked up to some girl—I'll call you back!"

During the talk-back, one of the basketball kids directs a question to Caleb, who plays Marcus. "Yo, bro, so in the play you were giving the other kid all kinds of shit for deep-throating that girl—and being like, *that's basically sexual assault*—"

Caleb: "Yeah."

Basketball Kid 5: "But, like, do you really believe that shit? Honestly?"

"Yeah, I do," Caleb says. "Listen, bro, you cannot force someone to do anything. You can't force a girl to kiss you or touch you or suck your dick. That's it. No question about it. Done. And I knew that when I started this project, but I didn't *know* that, you know what I'm saying? I didn't understand it and appreciate it the way I do now. Before doing this, bro, I probably would've asked the same question. But, uh, yeah, I one-hundred-percent believe that shit."

Basketball Kid 5: "Yeah, okay. I hear that. But could you get arrested for that shit?"

"Maybe. Maybe not," Caleb responds. "You trying to find out? Uh, no, right? Plus, it's about how you treat a person."

Basketball Kid 5 sits back in his seat and nods. Then: "Can I be in this play?"

Me: "Uh, sure. Do you act?"

Basketball Kid 5: "No . . . but I could."

2016: BOARDING SCHOOLS

In the wake of a sexual assault scandal at St. Paul's, several New England boarding schools invite us to their campuses. My assistant directors, Marquis Rodriguez and Charlotte Arnoux, and I walk the beautiful, college-like campuses of St. Paul's, Choate, and Andover. The schools are excited to receive us— their students had worked hard to bring us to their communities soon after the groundbreaking *Boston Globe* piece, "Private Schools, Painful Secrets."

And yet . . . there is definitely an air of defensiveness, one I've found to be common in my years of visiting high schools. Often, as I'm introduced to the student body, a good number of kids—most often the boys, to be honest—stare at me, stone-faced, like I'm there to inflict punishment. About two minutes into the play, though, they realize that's not true. The talk-backs are usually productive, even after the cold beginning.

In Connecticut, the standing ovations are passionate. The administration limits the talk-back to thirty-five minutes ("curfew"), so they're rushed—but still meaty. After one performance, a young woman raises her hand in the auditorium of seven hundred kids. "This play perfectly illustrates what's wrong with the world," she says. "Instead of teaching women not to get raped, we need to teach men not to rape."

There is applause from the seats. I nod. It's not the

first time I've heard this line. When the noise dies down, I conduct a live survey. "There are a lot of boys here. I have a question. How many of you have heard or been taught at some point in your life that it's wrong to rape someone?"

Can you guess how many hands went up?

All. Of. Them.

I continue, "Boys know they're not supposed to rape. Girls know they're not supposed to rape. Most people your age, no matter their gender, have been taught they're not supposed to rape. The problem is, we don't really know what that means. Our understanding of rape *and* our understanding of good, healthy sex are shaped by myths—the myth of the masked, armed, back-alley rapist; the myth of hardcore, no-really-means-yes, "sexy" (porn-influenced) sex; the myth that great boys can't also be rapists; the myth that boys can't be raped; the myth that "wetness" or an erection equals consent. The myth that it's easy to say what we want. It's our job, in spaces like this, to deconstruct these myths and to talk about reality."

The students break curfew and hover long after the show, waiting for their chance to talk to the boys and me. We stay for almost two hours each night, engaging, answering questions, sharing our frustrations with dismal sex-ed offerings, and dissecting the ridiculous "Tea" video, which many schools are showing to students in order to teach consent without actually talking about sex. GAH!

In Massachusetts, the atmosphere is more challenging. We're met with aggressive, even resentful audience members, which has the effect of making the talk-backs more valuable. A fourteen-year-old freshman stands up tall when I call on him. He projects his voice in the packed, four-hundred-seat theater like someone comfortable making themselves heard—which, as a teacher, I'm always excited to see.

Freshman: "Uh, you're a woman."

Me: ". . . Yes. That's true."

He looks over at his friends with a little smile and puff of breath. Then, "Have you ever identified as a man?"

Me: "No, I have not."

The freshman goes for it. No holding back. "Then what do you really know about being a guy that, you know, gives you *the right* to write this play?"

I watch some kids put their heads in their hands like, *Oh my God, this kid.* Some snicker into their fists. Some shake their heads like, *This is exactly why we need this play here.* But most just stare at me to see what I'll say.

Before I can answer, a girl stands, looking up at the freshman, who's sitting in the balcony, and says, "Men have been writing plays about women since the beginning of time. Do you really think she needs to explain herself?"

A ripple of gasps and murmurs through the theater. "I'm happy to explain myself," I offer. "Basically,

I was the one who was willing to listen. So, what gave me the right? This cast did. And so did all of the boys and men across the country who have shared their stories with me and expressed wanting to see something like *Now That We're Men*. I wrote it because I care about the experience you're living and I think other people should care, too. And I hope it rings true to you."

A lot of nodding heads. Then a hand shoots up, and an older boy stands. He's wearing one of the school's hockey sweatshirts, and immediately, before he can speak, kids start shouting his name, "Harrison!"

Harrison takes the mic being passed around. "What felt realistic to me was how drained you guys seemed by the end."

The actors nod. The audience seems puzzled.

Harrison: "I feel like that."

Silence.

"I feel like that all the time," Harrison says. "Basically, for me, it's a constant thing having to perform, I guess, and present a certain way, and puff up. And to act emotionally removed from things is a lot. And you guys seem very relaxed talking about this stuff and you seem calm. So, my question is, how can I be like that? How can we do that here?"

You could hear a pin drop. And then a kid yells (guttural, like he's in the Marines), "Harrison!"

The crowd begins to cheer as Fred answers him. "You *are* like that. Look what you just did. By being here in this room and talking with us. Saying the hard things. Being vulnerable and being real about patriarchy and gender expectations. Now, you just have to keep doing it."

2018: CHICAGO

We stage a sold-out run in Chicago at the famous Steppenwolf Theatre, produced by Ali Clark, Abby Pucker, Charlotte Arnoux, and me, with Marquis Rodriguez assistant-directing. We raise funds in order to offer 70 percent of every performance's tickets for free to school groups. We also arrange bus transportation to and from the theater.

In all my years in theater, I've never experienced audiences like we had at Steppenwolf. Most had never seen a play before. Many live less than thirty minutes from the theater, yet hadn't set foot in the building until *Now That We're Men*. The chatter each night is loud. Students dance in their seats to the pre-show music. They capture the experience on Instagram.

The cast takes the stage in character prior to the start of the play, to hang out like a group of friends during a free period in school. Caleb usually dances. In Chicago, audience members actually challenge him to a dance-off, right there on the stage. The excitement is palpable, but there are a few nights that I wonder whether the crowds will simmer down enough to get through the play. Without fail, the cast and the content grabs everyone's attention within minutes.

It's raw. Kids laugh when Andrew reveals he was assaulted as a child. Kids laugh and shout out *What's the problem?* when it's clear Nick raped his prom date. The kids talk to each other throughout the performance, trying to communally work out what they're seeing. After the curtain call following one of the most raucous performances, the boys and I are nervous to take the stage for the talk-back. I remind them that energized responses, like they'd been hearing throughout the whole show, are a part of catharsis. They nod. I say, "Stay calm and I'll wrap this up as soon as possible."

We take our seats and face the crowd. It's silent suddenly. All eyes on us. When I introduce myself—silence. When I talked about how the play came about—more silence. A few phones recording.

I ask if anyone has any thoughts or questions. Twenty hands shoot up in the air. The cast members and I eye each other. I pick a boy in the back row, who is now standing so he can see better.

Me: "Yes. Go for it."

The boy: "Who, me?"

Me: "Yup!"

The boy: "What is sexual assault?"

I peer at him and then glance around at the audience. No snickers. No stifled laughter. Just eyes on me, waiting for an answer. "Um . . . what do you mean, exactly?"

The boy, as open and vulnerable as I've ever seen anyone, says, "I mean, what is it? You said the play is about it a little bit ago, but what is it?"

"Thank you for asking that," I say. "How many people in this room have talked about sexual assault before?"

About three hands go up.

"Okay. Can one of you tell us what sexual assault is?"

A boy in the front row raises his hand. "Is it when you force a girl to have sex with you, or you have sex with her when she doesn't want you to? Or, like, just anything sexual without permission?"

Another boy raises a hand, but doesn't wait for me to call on him. "It can happen to boys, too. Even when they're young."

Silence.

He addresses Jordan, who plays Andrew. "Isn't that what was going on with your character? That woman raped him, right? And it's pretty fucked up because lots of times people act like it's cool to have sex when you're eleven or something—like, Chris Brown talks about that—but that's assault."

Jordan: "Yes."

Another boy leaning back in his chair chimes in. "Yo, when I was little, like every day my dad would be like 'You better not be a faggot.' And he'd tell me to fight people to prove I wasn't a pussy and not gay. Do you think your character's dad did that to him?"

"I don't think so," Jordan says. "But I think my character feels pressure from the world around him about what being a man is and he's frustrated that he doesn't feel like he fits the definition of what a man is supposed to be."

The boy lets his chair come back to earth. "Uh huh. Yeah. I feel that."

This particular talk-back lasts for almost an hour and a half. Audience members continue to share their own stories. We dive deep into conversations about what constitutes rape and sexual assault, the nuances around consent and body language, and the literal violence of being young and male today. These Chicago kids come back again and again to performances, texting, emailing, and DMing us for extra tickets or standing room. The artistic director of Steppenwolf says she's never seen anything like it.

At the last performance, I ask an audience member, who's returned to the show three times, why he keeps coming back. He says, "I like it. Like, that could be me up there. I never thought I liked plays. I always thought theater was mad corny and, like, not something I was into. But I think that's because it was never *for me* before, you know?"

I do know. *Now That We're Men* gives young men a chance to see themselves, their lives, and their friendships on stage. I hear it a lot. This is the thing that has moved the boys and me from the start.

2019: TEACHING *NTWM*

I sit across from fifty New York City public high school students in their overheated, overcrowded classroom. Some are clustered together on the floor, others tilt back in their chairs, all have well-worn copies of the acting edition of *Now That We're Men* in front of them. This is the first time the play has been incorporated into the English language arts curriculum in a public school anywhere in the U.S. I'm here to answer their questions. There are lots of hands in the air. I call on the seventeen-year-old boy in the back.

"What was the most challenging thing about writing this play?"

I get this question a lot during workshops or talkbacks following a performance. It's one of my favorites, because the answer is simple. "Everything," I say. It's true. As a teacher, writer, director, and activist, *everything* about this project was challenging.

He says, "Do you think it was even harder because you're a woman?"

I laugh. "Maybe, but also because I'm an adult. Also, because this was my first time writing male characters. It was a leap-of-faith creative experiment that required me to put *a* lot of things in check."

Another student shouts out, "Like what?"

"Well—" I hesitate. "I had to overcome the urge to 'mentor,' 'problem-solve,' and 'instruct.' Most adults can't resist moralizing teenagers—we want you to be who *we* want rather than who *you* are. I had to tell myself that you are complex human beings—just like we are."

They stare.

"And I had to check the assumptions I had about boys and boyhood," I say, "which were many. As a writer, my job was to bear witness to an experience I didn't know and then do my best to capture that experience as authentically and richly as possible. There were times when I was banging out this script at 3 a.m. in my living room, writing in the voices of sixteen-year-old boys, that I whispered to myself, 'I can't have him say this. I just can't.' And I'd remind myself, 'I *have* to have him say this because this is what he'd say—and if I pull punches, what's the point?' If you want to unpack something, you have to crack open the case. I really felt a responsibility to get it right."

A boy shouts out, "Responsibility to who?"

"To you. To the five high school boys who make up the cast. To the countless boys I've met across the country who've told me that what they're slogging through warrants care and attention. To the girls and gender non-conforming young people who are tired of bearing the burden of this conversation and cultural mess."

I call on a girl on the floor who is linking arms with her friend. "Do you think you care about boys more now?"

I think for a moment. "Look . . . I didn't grow up a boy. At this moment, I'm not the parent of a boy. I have a brother, who is a year younger and the great friend of my life. My favorite childhood buddy was a boy, who teased me for being a 'virgin' but also genuinely made me feel special. I grew up wilding around with twelve boy cousins. I was roofied by a guy. I locked myself in a strange bathroom and slept shivering on a bathmat in fear of a guy. I started a business with guys. I've lived with a guy for ten years. I'm raising a child with a guy. I've never, ever *cared* less than I do today—I just understand better today," I say, which gets to why I write plays. "Listening to each other and understanding each other more deeply helps us process our own experiences more fully."

"Do you ever get tired of talking to people our age about rape and this stuff?" the girl asks.

"No. Never. But we're talking about so much more than rape. We're talking about your ability to explore sex and seek pleasure safely. The conversation around consent doesn't always need to be connected to violence or aggression, it should also be about how to have sex that is fun for all involved."

They laugh.

"It's true. Healthy—even good—sex is a human right. You should fight for it and strive for it. This can't just be about how not to get hurt or in trouble, it has to be about how to enjoy it."

There is silence while they think about this, or maybe realize it for the first time. Then the girl's friend says, "And what are you hoping to achieve with your play?"

I toss it back to her. "What do you think I'm hoping to achieve?"

She looks at the floor, then at me. "This, I guess. All of us talking together like this. I've never talked about sex and power and assault and gender like this in school before, as part of a class."

"Yes. That's right," I say. "All of you here, right now, having a conversation like *this*, is exactly the goal."

The End

Contributors

CHARLOTTE ARNOUX hails from Marseille, France and works at the intersection of social justice and theater. She specializes in new works and has a passion for working with teens as a director, acting coach, teacher, and casting director. She is also the Managing Director of Katie Cappiello's GoodCapp Arts. charlottearnoux.com.

JENNIFER BAUMGARDNER is a writer and activist originally from Fargo. She is the publisher of Dottir Press, author of several books about feminism including *Manifesta* and *Look Both Ways: Bisexual Politics*, and the director of the documentaries *It Was Rape* and *I Had an Abortion*.

SKULI BAUMGARDNER is a high school freshman in Manhattan. He plays bass guitar and ukulele.

COOPER LEE BOMBARDIER is a writer and visual artist originally from New England, currently residing in Halifax, Canada. He has toured with the spoken word phenomenon Sister Spit and is the author of *Pass with Care: Memoirs*.

TARIQ CRABBE was born in Brooklyn and raised in New Jersey. After high school, he founded and toured with the Voices of Promise choir. He attended John Jay College of Criminal Justice—following a period of dropping in and out of college due to financial struggles—and graduated with a Bachelor's degree in Criminal Justice in 2016.

JORDAN ELIOT is an actor who played Andrew in the original 2016 production of *Now That We're Men*. He attends New York University: Tisch School of the Arts, where is studying Drama and Psychology.

EVE ENSLER is a playwright, performer, and activist best known for her play *The Vagina Monologues* and V-Day, a global movement to end violence against women. She ho-created the One Billion Rising global campaign and City of Joy.

DOMINIC FUMUSA has had leading roles on *Homeland, Sex and the City, The Sopranos, Bones*, and is best known for playing Kevin Peyton on Showtime's *Nurse Jackie*. Fumusa's extensive stage experience includes originating roles in the New York premieres of Sarah Ruhl's *Stage Kiss* and *Passion Play*, Richard Greenberg's Tony-winning *Take Me Out*, and Stephen Belber's plays *The Power of Duff, Fault Lines,* and *Tape*.

CALEB GRANDOIT originated the part of Marcus in *Now That We're Men*. He is an actor, dancer, writer, and senior at the College of Staten Island. His credits include editing the original student plays *Intersections* and *Security Strike* (dir. By Kamilah Forbes) at Opening Act's Annual Play Reading at New World Stages.

ANASTASIA HIGGINBOTHAM is the creator of the critically acclaimed Ordinary Terrible Things children's series, which includes *Divorce Is the Worst*; *Death Is Stupid*; *Tell Me about Sex, Grandma;* and *Not My Idea: A Book About Whiteness*.

ALPHONSO JONES II originated the role of Evan in *Now That We're Men*. He is a sophomore student at St. Peter's University and pursuing a career in the entertainment industry.

LOUIS J LEVIN grew up in London and moved to New York aged fifteen. He is currently a junior at the University of Chicago, majoring in Interdisciplinary Studies in the Humanities with a focus on fashion. He's a member of a fraternity and also teaches yoga in his spare time.

CHE LUXENBERG attends Blue School in New York. He loves to act and has trained as an actor at the Lee Strasberg Institute, as well as GoodCapp Arts.

JACQUELINE LUXENBERG, born and raised in New York, has worked in different areas of fashion. Her thirteen-year-old son, Che, is her best friend.

JUSTICE NNANNA is an artist and activist based in Brooklyn and Lagos. He graduated from New York University and studied at the Royal Academy of Dramatic Arts (RADA). Through his film and photo work, he explores ways of seeing social-political spaces and nonverbal methods of communicating the human experience.

ALEX PARRISH is a stage performer, musical theater composer, and voice teacher whose work explores the moral ambiguities and intricate patterns of day-to-day life. He lives in New York City.

PETER QUALLIOTINE co-founded the Organization for Prostitution Survivors (OPS) in Seattle with Noel Gomez in 2012. Peter is a founding co-chair and sits on the executive committee of World Without Exploitation.

CARMEN JULIA REYES is an English teacher at Millennium High School in Manhattan. She resides in Brooklyn with her loving family.

RAYSHAWN RICHARDSON originated the role of Derek in *Now That We're Men*. He currently studies Finance at New York University while simultaneously auditioning for television roles. Recently, he played Jared in the Netflix film *See You Yesterday*.

MARQUIS RODRIGUEZ is an actor and teacher known for playing Raymond Santana in Ava DuVernay's *When They See Us*, and for starring in the upcoming *Game of Thrones* prequel. He has previously worked with both *SLUT: The Play* and *Now That We're Men* performing spoken word poetry at talkbacks.

ISIAH ROSA is a sophomore at New York University: Tisch School of the Arts and is pursuing a BFA in Game Design.

WILLIAM UPBIN attends the University of Pennsylvania. He is majoring in Economics, minoring in Music History, and is a member of Penn's fencing team.

PRIYANKA VORUGANTI is a poet, actress, and feminist in New York City. She attends Horace Mann and is a part of *SLUT: The Play,* as well as a staff writer for *Speciwoman Magazine*.

Acknowledgments

Thank you to Jamison and our curious, joyful daughter, Francesca ("Francie"), who was just a dream when I wrote this play.

Thank you to all the great men in my family—especially my devoted, impassioned dad, Mike, and my cherished brother and best friend, Jim—who always strive to demonstrate vulnerability, strength, kindness, and feminism: Sho, Tommy, Jeremy, Gregg, Ean, Adrian, Jordan, Brenden, Eric, Matt, Dan, and Jeff.

To my creative collaborators who make me a better teacher, writer, thinker, activist, listener, and friend, day in and day out: Marquis Rodriguez, Mike Turner, Adrian Burke, and Daniel Melnick.

To my mom, Jane. My soul sister from day one.

To my grandmothers, Helen and Kay. I miss them dearly and take risks in their honor every day.

To my teachers, especially Penny Aschuler, Susan Szachowicz, Bill Szachowicz, Jim Burley, Carol Thomas, Theresa Capachione, Dori Bryan-Ployer, Penny Knight, Bill Balzac, and Geoffrey Horne.

To the Brockton High School Drama Club—my favorite place during my teen years.

To my loyal circle of friends and colleagues: Suzan Etkin, Stella Fitzgerald, Nancy Chilton, Ali Chilton, Marcela Barry, Nicolette Donen, Lauren Hersh, Rachel Foster, Yasmeen Hassan, and Elizabeth Kling.

To Jennifer Baumgardner, my dear friend and a personal hero, who encourages me to jump off cliffs time and time again. You are the best (most patient!!) editor and publisher I could ask for.

To Alice Stewart, Noelle McManus, Larissa Pienkowski, Kait Heacock, and Drew Stevens, for being part of Team Dottir Press and producing this book.

To Charlotte Arnoux and Alessandra Clark—the smartest, most determined, most resourceful and daring people I know. Thank you for having my back and for inspiring me 24/7.

To Jordan Eliot, Caleb Grandoit, Rayshawn Richardson, Fred Hechinger, and Alphonso Jones, for your bravery, openness, radiance, and friendship.

And finally, to all my students. I am endlessly grateful for the opportunity to learn from you. Thank you for welcoming me into your lives, your worlds, and your stories.

KATIE CAPPIELLO is a feminist teacher, writer, director, and producer who uses cultural expression to transform rape culture. Her plays include *Keep Your Eyes Open*; *Facebook Me*; *A Day in the Life*; *SLUT: The Play*; and *Her Story, Uncut*. She co-edited *SLUT: A Play and Guidebook for Combating Sexism and Sexual Violence* (Feminist Press, 2015). She lives in Brooklyn. Her Netflix original series debuts in 2020 and intersects with the themes in this book and all of her plays.